21 Powerful Money Secrets to AWAKEN THE MILLIONAIRE WITHIN

Being in your
9 to 5 Job

R SUBRAMANYA CFP[CM]

ABUNDANCE INDIA

STARDOM BOOKS

WORLDWIDE

www.StardomBooks.com

STARDOM BOOKS

A Division of Stardom Publishing

and infoYOGIS Technologies.

105-501 Silverside Road

Wilmington, DE 19809

FIRST EDITION MAY 2018

Stardom Books

21 Powerful Money Secrets to
Awaken the Millionaire Within

Being in your
9 to 5 Job

R Subramanya CFP^{CM}

p. cm.

Category: Self-help/Business/Finance

ISBN-13: 978-1-7323287-0-9

ISBN-10: 1-7323287-0-6

DEDICATION

This book is dedicated to my parents and many of my Gurus, particularly M. Gopalakrishnan, my in-laws, my wife & children, my brother-in-law Sathi, his wife Latha, my sister Manjula, my brother-in-law C Subramani, my younger sister Jayanthi, my brothers Rajan & Saravanan, my friends J M Santiago, Shanbagh, Lodha, Anandkumar, Vinod Kumar, my young friend Shree Uday, my BNI friends and all my clients and well-wishers.

TABLE OF CONTENTS

ACKNOWLEDGMENTS

It's remarkable that this is my first book.

After over forty years of learning, teaching and training other individuals and entrepreneurs on how to generate more money and manage it efficiently to accelerate the process of creating wealth, this is my first book. I'm finally "eating my own cooking," as Keith Cunningham says.

As I sat down to write this Acknowledgment section, I knew then, as I still do now, that I'm leaving hundreds of people out who deserve recognition for my progress and success. It's impossible to thank everyone who has impacted the development of this book. So if you don't see your name listed below, I apologize to you in advance, and I hope you reach out so then I can thank you personally.

As I said in the opening page, this book is dedicated to my Guru M. Gopalakrishnan, my family and my well-wishers who helped and supported me to become the person that I am today.

I do owe the great Chanakya a quick "Thank You," because his teachings have greatly inspired and influenced me in my financial well-being.

To my mother, Radhamma and my father Rajagopal, thank you for bringing me into this beautiful and abundant world to play the game of life. Although I was losing in the early part of my life, every failure taught me something valuable and delivered unforgettable lessons that made me what and who I am today.

To my life partner, Chitra Subramanya, who is like the rudder of my ship that sets sail each day to explore new territories of understanding, both personally and professionally. Thank you again, Chitra; I love you.

To my children, Sangeetha, Shalini, Venkatesh Kumar and Haritha for their unconditional love and continuous support throughout.

To my son-in-law Prem, who is very supportive and has been there for me always.

To my father-in-law, Venugopal, and mother-in-law Bhagyavathi, who stood by me during my difficulties.

To my brother-in-law and sister, whom I can never appreciate enough Sathi and Latha.

To my sisters Manjula & Jayanthi and my brothers Rajan and Saravanan for their support.

To all my beloved members of BNI Excellence, past and present, who are highly benevolent and have been helpful in my growth.

To my friends, J M Santiago, Shanbagh, CR Lodha, ST Anandkumar, Vinod kumar and Shree Uday who had extended their support when I most needed it.

To all my clients who have become an integral part of this big family.

To Raam Anand & his team from Stardom Alliance for their timely support in publishing my book.

And finally, I write these words to appreciate you, the reader. Without you, the contents of this book would be far less relevant to the world, because all 21 Money secrets would still be in my head.

I hope our paths cross often and I hope that you keep up with the social conversation on our Facebook Community at https://www.facebook.com/SubbuCFP.

"21 powerful money secrets to AWAKEN THE MILLIONAIRE WITHIN Being in your 9 to 5 job"

Foreword-A Wake-Up Call

"In the absence of wake-up calls,
many of us never really confront
the critical issues of financial life."
- Anonymous

On May 14, 2010, Friday morning, my client, Raghuram (I call him Raghu) CEO of an MNC, called me to check if I was free for a discussion. I asked him what the matter was. He, in a very urgent tone said, "I'd like to discuss this in person rather than on phone, Sir." Understanding the urgency, I agreed to meet him at 5 the same evening.

What Raghu told me was shocking. One of his deputies aged 38 years had committed suicide by jumping from the 7th floor of his office. He was married - had two daughters who were studying in a convent. He was a brilliant man, very efficient and adored by all. But now, dead.

What really shocked everyone was partly his death but mostly the reason that unveiled itself on his death. No one knew about this. Not his friends, not his family. Hell, not even his wife.

For several years, he had been rolling over credit card and personal loans. He had notched up close to Rs 40 L in debt.

One of his colleagues found a suicide note which said that he was taking this extreme step as he could no longer face the debtors who were constantly harassing him. He specifically addressed his wife saying, 'Dear, I am terribly sorry for doing this to you'. Even I didn't know I was ₹40 Lakhs in debt until all of them came knocking at our door.

This is just one of the countless cases in our society.

The question one must ask oneself is – WHY DO PEOPLE GET TRAPPED IN DEBT? So deep that they themselves don't realise; so trapped that they can find no way out.

Until recently, the Indian middle class contained highly conservative borrowers. With a strong cultural aversion to loans and with very little finance on the market, most people lived frugally all their lives.

Easy money through credit cards and loans flooded into the markets by foreign banks and institutions to brain wash people to develop spending habits that eventually led to Global economic crunch.

According to industry reports, the amount of outstanding credit card debt in India tripled between 2004 and 2007. Private and foreign banks marketed credit cards and loans to consumers by creating needs in the minds of people who had no experience of borrowing.

Few years back getting credit cards in India was very easy. some even thought having multiple credit cards added to their "cool" quotient. Little did they know that they were digging their financial grave.

It is a vicious cycle. First, people are made to want a better lifestyle by dangling fancy things before their eyes. Then, they are provided with easy money in the form of loans through credit cards, instalment schemes, personal loans, etc. to make these unnecessary things affordable. Thus started the cycle of people buying things they don't need with the money they don't have to please people who don't even matter.

Individuals are directly or indirectly driven towards consumerism and there is no way one can escape this vicious circle unless he has a strong financial education that can protect him from cunning marketers and product pushers.

People don't realise that easy money is actually more expensive - it pushes one into debt trap for a life time.

Hence I made this my mission – to educate people about money and help them live a life of their dreams. I, having been a victim of debt myself, know how helpless and hopeless one must feel. I know the struggle it takes to get out as well. It left such a huge mark in my life that I was determined to find the easiest, fastest and most effective way out.

I have been helping and guiding individuals for many years now. But each time, it was only one person or a group of people that I could reach out to. But I wanted to reach out to multitudes. Therefore I started writing articles in newspapers and magazines and even wrote blogs. Even after all this, I felt there was potential to reach out to a bigger mass. From that thought, this book was born.

This book contains proven, time-tested actionable yet simple principles that can help and guide any individual to a financially stress free life.

I am pretty sure your eyes just drifted past the above four words. Take a minute and read each word there. You will then understand how powerful these principles are.

Remember, THERE IS NO SUCH THING AS POVERTY IN GOD'S LAND. God did not create poverty. Among the myriad unnecessary things that man created, poverty tops the list. If I was to explain poverty in a sentence, I would say – "*Poverty is the result of ignorance*".

This book not only gives you clarity on this aspect but also equips you with actionable tools and techniques to guard yourself against all possible financial threats.

Here's wishing you from the bottom of my heart a life full of "Joy & Freedom".

INTRODUCTION

1

Shame! I took 48 years to find my freedom!

"If I can do it, you can do it too!"
- R Subramanya CFP

17th April 1966, a Sunday afternoon I was playing with my friends near my house. Back then, there were only a few houses scattered all over. I was living with my parents and three siblings in a place called Ramamurthy Nagar.

It was a vast open plateau. My house could be seen from almost a kilometre. There were two huge lakes-one on the eastern side of my house and the other towards the south-west. We had a full view of the banks of both lakes with a line-up of trees. A narrow mud road was the only main road that was connecting ITI colony and other nearby villages.

As I was playing, I saw a short, thin man with two well-built men walking on the bank of the south-western lake. Initially, I ignored them and continued playing. But, after a while I was sure they were walking towards my house, crossing the paddy fields. I quickly ran to my house and informed my father who was busy reading a weekly magazine. He dropped the magazine to the floor at just my description of the man.

He came out and on seeing the stranger, he froze. I could see his face turning pale. He looked at my sister and me as though he didn't want us to know what was happening. My father walked up to the stranger and said, "Champak Sahib, please give me 2 minutes, I will get dressed, and we can go to the banyan tree and discuss" trying to prevent him from entering our house.

But, the visitor was curt. He said sternly, "Discuss what?" I saw my father shudder. The short man went on, "Rajagopal, I have come here to get you and your family out of this house. It now belongs to me."

My father began to plead him. "Champak Sahib, I know I have not paid you for eight months, please give me some more time, I will settle all the dues."

Champak said, "I have given you more time than I normally do but you failed. Now move out with your family. You have taken me for granted. I will show you who I am."

By then my mother, who was listening to the conversation came out, spread a mat on the floor and requested the visitors to come in and sit. After a moment's hesitation, the three men conceded. My mother offered them buttermilk and asked them to wait to say she would get back with the money. That calmed them down a little.

Once out of earshot, she whispered to me to bring my grandparents who stayed close by. I quickly ran to them and told them what was happening and ran back home. On my return, I found a mob of curious neighbors gaping at my house, only adding to the embarrassment of the situation.

My mother quickly took me to a pawn broker's shop and pledged her jewels to get some money. Back home, she called my father and grandparents inside for a discussion. Then, she handed over the money to my father and told him to give it to Champak Lal and request for three more months.

Long story short, my parents eventually sold the house and settled all the dues to Champak Lal.

What I felt then cannot be expressed in words. We were homeless, helpless and vulnerable.

That night I couldn't sleep. But, I knew one thing for sure- I wasn't ever going to live such a mediocre life, physically or financially. Seeing my father shiver with fear, my mother hold back her tears as she pledged the last piece of jewelry she owned, their faces when we sold our only house - I knew. I knew then that I wasn't ever going let money get the better of me. I would never become its slave. I was determined to find a way out.

Like Paulo Coelho said in his book, "The Alchemist," when you are determined to do something, the whole universe conspires to help you." And the universe did conspire to help me.

When something is set in your mind, you start to correlate everything happening around you and convince yourself that it's a good omen, a sign from God. I did the same. All of this pain and struggle never let me sleep at night. So one day, while watching a movie, I saw a young boy about my age, lose his parents. He worked his way to freedom and helped his sister from the clutches of her evil in-laws. On a normal day, it would have made no difference. But that day, given the temperament I was in, it gave me the strength and belief that I can overcome the current situation too.

All this while, I felt trapped in poverty, sufferings, and humiliation. And now, a tiny seed of richness, confidence, and courage was sown in my mind. I looked up, broadened my shoulders and told myself aloud–"One day I will be rich."

Life was, as it always is, tough. Every step of the way, there was a hurdle. But I wasn't perturbed. My determination never died. My eyes were set on the goal. After my education, I got a placement in a German Company. Even though I was earning a decent salary compared to my peers, I was always short of money because I still lived on borrowings. Being the eldest in the family, I had to shoulder a lot of responsibilities. I had no option but to borrow on high rates of interest. Or so I thought.

Years passed. I earned some. I borrowed most. And I spent all.

Before sleeping each day, I used to wonder if I would ever reach financial stability considering how things were going. My father borrowed money. Now, I was borrowing money. If

I wasn't doing anything different, how would I end up in any different a situation? That bothered me. I knew I had to change something but I didn't know what. I was desperate.

I began each day with the hope that something new would happen. And one day, it did. I was given the assignment to design and develop an automatic feeding system for a power press.

On reaching to the shop floor, I studied the press and was then introduced to the planner who was managing the press shop. It was a very challenging job and the person who was handling it earlier had given up on the project.

It was sheer luck that I was assigned that project.

God has blessed me with a strong ability - Creativity. In situations where people saw problems, I saw solutions. Within two days, I was able to solve the issue. My boss and the end users were ecstatic that not only did I complete the task but I finished it fast. I became a star. My visibility in the company increased and more challenging projects came my way. I succeeded in all of them one by one which made me very popular among the top-level officials in the company.

During that time Gopalakrishnan, the man who was in charge of the presses, became my friend. Later in the book, you will get to know that he eventually became my mentor and my Guru who was instrumental in changing my life forever.

One of those days while having lunch, I confided in him about the other side of my life. He listened to me patiently and told me not to worry about it and gave me the confidence that I would come out of it soon.

The next day, I met him at his office for a routine meeting. After the meeting, he called me to a side and gave me a bundle of cash and said that he had saved it for the future and as he didn't have any immediate need for it, he'd like me to have it. I was overwhelmed. I was really in need of cash. I was hesitant but he insisted that I take it.

I cleared off my debt using that cash. I was so relieved that that night I slept like a baby knowing no one would knock at my door in the middle of the night asking for their money. What Gopalakrishnan did was so selfless. He gave me the money with absolutely no idea whether he would get it back or not. My respect for him grew by multitudes.

We started meeting more often. Slowly he understood my difficulties, took a special interest in me and started guiding me. He'd always tell me that my strength was innovative automation and that I should explore the outside world for new opportunities because companies were facing significant challenges in their manufacturing plants and Automation was the key.

I started looking around, visited industrial areas, met and discussed with a lot of people. Slowly things started moving. Initially, I got only small projects. Since I was strong in my field, I used to come out with instant solutions. People started talking about me. They would say if you have a technical problem and if you are unable to solve it, call Mr. Subramanya. I started getting additional income off it. Soon, another seed of prosperity was sown in my mind.

Thus, my financial situation started to improve. My Guru introduced me to a French Company who were facing numerous technical challenges in their manufacturing unit. On visiting them, I came to know that my Guru had already established some groundwork. In the very first meeting itself, they handed over the project to me. "We have heard a lot about you, Mr. Subramanya. We are happy to be working with you." they said. It made me feel excellent about myself and motivated me to do even better.

When the CEO of the Company came to visit the newly completed system, he was fascinated by how I had steered away from the normal standards and created a better and more efficient design. A few days later, I got a call from the CEO's assistant. She asked if I was free to meet with the CEO. I thought it was another job and said yes gladly. But, that wasn't the case.

He asked me to take a seat. He looked very serious – like he meant some serious business. I started to wonder if I had made any errors in my design. His next sentence proved me wrong. "Would you like to join our company as the Vice President, Mr. Subramanya?" he asked. Lost in my reverie, I thought I misheard him and said, "Pardon me, Sir." And he repeated it.

I was stunned, shocked, happy and hysterical all at the same time.

But mostly, I was thrilled to see what was in store for me. My experience had taught me that the outside world brims with opportunities. It just takes the right set of eyes to identify and capitalize. I wanted to leverage my creativity even more rather than restricting myself to one company.

I politely refused the offer promising him that I, with my team, would support him if need be.

I quit my German company. I didn't have a plan yet. But I knew that as long as I had a safety net, I wouldn't care about the jump. I was confident that this would turn out good but I had nothing to substantiate before my family. Therefore, for almost three months, my family remained in the dark and had no idea that I had quit my first job.

Soon, I set up an engineering industry dealing in industrial automation. With the help of Guru, my team, my customers, and well-wishers, I steadily grew.

After about five years, when I checked my records, reality hit me. I had an incredible inflow but an outrageous outflow. A lot of money was flowing in, yes. And a lot of money was flowing out too. But I didn't know where all of it was going. I had no control over my finances. That's when I realized that I was like a vital conduit through which money was just flowing out.

I discussed with my Guru and decided to meet my chartered accountant to seek his help in planning my finances. Back then, I was unaware of money, how it worked, how to manage and how to create assets, etc. I was of the opinion that it was a chartered accountant's area. Not an ordinary man's.

I discussed with my Chartered Accountant regarding this but wasn't satisfied with his reply. He told me where my money went but he didn't say how to plan and manage it, how to stop it from happening the next time. This would help me only after the storm has passed. It won't help me protect myself from the storm.

I needed answers. So I met different people, read many books, attended discussions. But no one gave me a satisfactory answer. Since no one could give me the answer I sought, I decided to find it by myself.

That marked the start of my research. I observed people, individuals, business owners, etc. and to my surprise, I found that about 90% of people are facing one or another type of financial challenge.

They all had a striking similarity. Outwardly, each of them appeared vibrant and comfortable. In fact, they were conditioned to pretend and behave as if they were luxurious and comfortable. But in reality, they were far from it. Everyone just wanted to look better in the eyes of others. What they saw when they looked in the mirror didn't matter. What others thought of them mattered more than what they thought of themselves. Some even felt happy when others envied their fake-riches.

I sat and pondered over why such multitudes were afflicted with the same disease. I traced the line all the way back to its roots – our education system. Our education system never touched upon anything related to money management. Every teacher told us, "Son, if you don't study well, you won't get a good job, and if you don't get a good job, you won't earn well." Everyone spoke about "earning" money. No one spoke about "managing" it. Our family, friends, and society always told us to "save" money for the future. No one said, "Invest" money for your future. Therefore, we were pre-conditioned this way even without realizing. And when someone says otherwise about money, we are reluctant to accept it.

Having understood the situation, I consciously started my journey of lifetime financial education. I learned a lot from various people, read a lot of books, got certified as a financial planner, and I began my journey towards economic freedom.

It was tough and I had to do it on trial and error basis. I was my first client. I did all experiments on myself and my family members. I made several mistakes and lost a lot of money, had a roller coaster ride with five significant dips in life. Each was more severe than the previous. But as they say, when you learn something the hard way, it'll be etched in your memory forever.

The fifth was the worst. I lost everything and became bankrupt due to a business deal with a reputed company. After having been hit by four groundbreaking storms, luckily my mentor needed some machinery and gave me a big order.

A few envious and corrupt officials did not like me as I didn't align with their thoughts and ideologies. They were waiting for my mentor to retire and once he did, they targeted me by revoked the bank guarantee and collected all the money from my bank. All our supplies were rejected, our orders cancelled and all payments stopped. It was a devastating loss.

I still remember the day when the bank manager called. I kept looking at the phone hoping he would cut before I answered. But, no. I answered and he said, "Mr. Subramanya, the inevitable has happened. Your customer has revoked the bank guarantee and we are bound to honor it. You do not have even a single penny in your account. You will have to repay us at the earliest or we shall be forced to press legal charges." The entire world was on pause. These words kept echoing in my ears. I could hear my heartbeat. I don't think I heard anything the manager said after that.

I went back home. Looking at me, my wife asked, "What happened?" I couldn't even get myself to look her in the eye. I looked at the floor and said, "We have lost everything." I choked. She came towards me, sat on the floor, looked up at me and asked, "What happened?"

I told her everything. As I was talking to her, I relived every moment before my eyes, and I started to understand what I could've done differently. I was able to identify my mistakes and a better way to do it if I had to do it again. Having let it all out, I stood up and realized that things weren't so bad. My wife hugged me tight and said, "When we started, we started with nothing and grew this much. We will do it again, but this time we will do it right."

I nodded. The best part about hitting rock bottom was it can only get better from here on out.

Again, my Guru, Gopalakrishnan, came to my rescue. He lent me money to pay salaries and other expenses to keep my business running. He had given me close to 17 lakhs without even a signature or security of any kind. He was an angel in disguise. Had he not done what he did for me, I wouldn't be sitting here writing this book.

Anyway, I managed to keep my business running. The next three years were very crucial. One wrong step and I'd go back to square one.

So, I was very cautious. With the support of my Guru Gopalakrishnan, my wife Chitra, her brother Sathyanarayana (my brother-in-law) and his wife Latha and my entire team of employees, I was able to regain all that I had lost.

This entire journey was life-changing. I noticed that I no longer enjoyed managing my industry. I made an exit plan of 3 years. Divided my company into five parts and handed them over to my employees who stood by me during the time of crisis.

My research showed that 9 out of 10 people had money problems. And as long as money existed, so would the problems.

There were many people to create machinery. If not me, there's always another person. But not many to teach you about money. So I made it my life's mission to help people come out of money problems. The vital and practical lessons that I learned over all those years helped me attain my financial freedom on my 48th Birthday. It also provided me with the right skills and tools to help others achieve their financial independence in the easiest, fastest and most efficient way.

I believe that with financial education and proper guidance one can live a spectacular life – a life of their dreams. This belief & my success gave me my purpose. What I started as a mere hobby became my passion. Soon, my passion became my profession. Someone rightly said, "Make your passion your profession, and you won't have to work even a single day."

I started off by helping my friends and relatives. Soon, the word spread and more people started to approach me. Seeing the transformation in their lives gave me an immense sense of satisfaction.

To me, financial education is a noble profession, and my heart and soul is in it.

I continually update myself in the financial domain. With over four decades of experience, I have developed several games and activities to help people understand their financial world better. When I say "Learn," people shy away saying, "I need a break from this. I have been working all week." But when I say "playing," they spring up with unbounded energy. These games that I have created playfully teach you the seriousness of your financial situation.

Our "Money Game Mastery" (MGM) programs have helped thousands of people attain financial freedom not only in India but overseas as well.

I believe that life is a gift from God and every individual has the right and freedom to make the most of it. Unfortunately, the knowledge that is imparted to us right from our childhood days is entirely unsupportive and prepares us to be better and better slaves serving somebody instead of living a life of our dreams. We are caught up in the rat race and have absolutely no time, no knowledge, no guidance and no opportunity in sight for a life of our dreams. Sadly most people remain being slaves throughout their lives and take their dreams to their graves. With financial education and proper guidance, one can quickly attain financial freedom and lead a fabulous life.

2

THERE IS NO POVERTY IN GOD'S LAND!

"See yourself living in Abundance and you will attract it. It works every time, with every person."
- Bob Proctor.

Every morning, before I open my eyes, I say a short prayer of gratitude. Diagonal to my bed, there is a long window which opens directly to the sky with no buildings obstructing my view. I go out to the terrace and watch the break of dawn. As the first rays of the sun make its way across the vast sky, the birds start to chirp. The leaves of the tree glisten in the sunlight. I stand there and take one long deep breath. The smell of the fresh unpolluted air, wow. What a creation! What a blessing! What God created for us is a paradise. It knows no sorrow, no hatred, no greed. He has blessed us with things galore. He has given us the freedom to reap the benefits of his beautiful creation.

God created everything in abundance. The air that we breathe, water that we consume, land that we are living on, the trees, plants, mountains, and rivers are all in abundance. If you take a minute, you shall realize that we can't even fully comprehend the size and magnitude of all the natural resources we are blessed with.

We see a countless number of creatures that tread this earth. They all take birth, go through their life cycle and finally depart, just like humans. God has provided equal rights to all.

To you, reader, I pose a straightforward question. Who, other than a human needs money?

Have we at any time seen or heard of an animal approaching someone asking for money?

Whatever a living being requires for its life has already been created in this world by the Almighty. Whatever we need for today, tomorrow and the rest of our lives has already been created by God. In case, the supreme power wants to grant a thousand of years of life for all of us, even then, we have enough resources to cater to all our needs.

But, what do we see? A section of people, to retain power in their own hands, have brought in "money" to promote subordination and slavery. They have, in the name of civilization, brought in money as a barrier between man and everything else in this world.

I usually ask people if they can think of any five situations in their life when life can go on without money. Although initially, they believe it to be a simple task, they eventually find themselves at a loss.

We live in a strange world. Even though God has provided everything free of cost, nothing is free today. The times are changing and are becoming more difficult by the day. It is a vast and complex system which you and I cannot change. The only way is to evaluate and understand the situation is such a way that we don't get victimized. Use the positives to our advantage and insulate ourselves from the negatives.

How do we do that? We must learn and adapt.

Unfortunately, our schools and colleges do not teach us this. If we notice, every sphere of our life has achieved vast advancements in multiple fields. To explain better - take any area, so much research is carried out, new things are emerging. They are all being documented and implemented in the education system. But, why not financial literacy for ordinary people like you and me?

The reason is quite simple. A section of wealthy people, to retain power, conveniently keep financial literacy out of our education system. It took me over four decades to understand this.

Although slavery and bonded labor were abolished decades ago, slavery of the mind due to money remains. It's distressing to see innocent people struggle and continue to lead a life of slavery until their end.

Like I always say, God has given us everything in abundance. But, because of a section of selfish people, the suffering continues in many lives. With proper education and understanding of the way money works, one can undoubtedly lead a spectacular life.

Let us all work towards eradicating poverty of all kinds, from the surface of this planet. I have begun my journey, and I request you all to join hands with people like me and support this cause.

3

SLOW POISON

***"In the absence of clearly-defined goals,
we become strangely loyal to performing daily trivia
until ultimately we become enslaved by it".***
- Robert A.Heinlein

Today's young and salaried people are experiencing multiple problems. Why? It is because of one missing aspect of life called financial literacy that is conveniently being ignored. People are jump starting their life without experience or guidance. They try to observe others and copy their money behaviours which may or may not be right as no two individuals will have the same situation. They learn by trial and error. People, who are ignorant themselves financially are leading the others. It's like "Blind leading the Blind".

Any experiment with money is expensive and cannot be easily reversed. What starts as a small and manageable inconvenience gets bigger and bigger which then becomes unmanageable leading to financial stress. It is like taking poison every day.

Individuals with the help of their aspiring parents complete their college hoping for a great life. But, the reality is that, they get trapped in a maze with no clue of getting out.

It hurts me to see millions of youngsters fall prey to wrong advice and end up being slaves to banks, Insurance companies and other agencies for most part of their productive life. I am committed to my cause of spreading awareness among youngsters to customize their lives such that they can aim for early retirement. This book is the tool I wish to use to reach out to millions and change their lives. If you read it carefully you will have answers to all your problems. I have carefully selected two case studies to spread a part of my message to the readers.

Anil, a salaried young man who found himself in a debt trap was experiencing severe financial stress. He had lost interest in his job, his company and in life. With proper guidance and strategies he could get out of such a miserable life to find his freedom within an unbelievably short period of 4 years. Yes. You read it right, it is four years.

Surprisingly, Anil is the first guy from among my clientele to gain his financial independence in such a short period of time.

How it happened is discussed in the later part of the book starting from Golden Rule 18 under Outer Game of Money.

Ganesh, another salaried young man was fortunate that he could get proper guidance at the right time to gain his financial freedom within 10 years of being in his 9 to 5 job.

It is as simple as that. Financial education is the key.

Following are few pain points (Slow Poison) which are being experienced by the salaried people.

- There is generally no clarity about money and budget creation.
- They don't know where their money is going.
- They believe that borrowing is the only option and end up in a debt trap. Eventually, they become victims of money with a mountain of debt to clear.
- If they have parents facing health issues, there exists no source for emergency funds.
- A lack of knowledge about financial management which stems from not knowing how to save or invest and also not knowing where they can safely place their money and whom to trust with it.
- Most are only looking for instant gratification.
- A herd mentality usually exists where they tend to follow what they hear from others and don't perform their own research. Greed to bleed.
- A tendency to live from pay-cheque to pay-cheque arises.
- Due to the sudden inflow of money, most don't pay enough attention to their spending habits and peer pressure may make them spend more than they normally would have.
- Because of excessive spending patterns, they get used to credit cards and loans.
- The belief that earning more will solve all problems hence always look for ways to earn fast cash.
- The inability to be far sighted often leads to a lack of responsibility for tomorrow's needs.

Salaried Class:

- There tends to be no clarity in money management amongst couple.
- The lack of communication between them where they don't believe that their partner can question their spending patterns and hence a secretive nature develops.
- Investing in semi furnished/ unfurnished/ project delay flats. They are in a situation with one foot on either side. On one side, they pay EMI's and on the other, they will have to pay rentals as well.
- Investing in speculative markets.
- Couples having individual goals, almost always leads to issues. They don't manage money together and it leads to financial problems in the future.
- A lack of trust exists when it comes to matters of money.
- They may have different levels of financial education. Although, it becomes the responsibility of the one with more knowledge to educate the lesser education.
- Busy lifestyle (hectic work-schedule) that sucks away all the time and energy forcing people to ignore money management completely.
- Buying excessive and unnecessary life insurance products and properties assuming them to be good investments and eventually becoming slaves to banks and other lending agencies.

Slow Poison:

Uneven Spending - The tendency to spend on wants is greater in the beginning of the month when salary is credited and this impulsive spending leads to a situation where one is unable to meet basic needs.

- Use of Credit Cards with Limits above their Income.
- No track of where the money is spent.
- No allocation for the budget of the month.
- No provision or allocation is made for the taxes to be paid (cases other than salary) - advance taxes are not paid and usually the taxes for one Financial Year are paid from the income of the next Financial Year i.e. from the Assessment Year's income.
- Unplanned Big Expenditures - Usually due to peer pressure or as matter of pride, people tend to buy items of luxury such as a Car, Phone etc using a credit facility which are beyond their powers to repay comfortably.
- No planning before taking a credit/loan- to ensure they are repaid without disrupting basic financial needs.
- Failure to discuss Finances with spouse/family - They will limit their wants only if they understand the financial position of the family.
- Savings not equals Investment - People generally retain large sums of money in savings accounts to satisfy a falsified sense of security.
- Blind assumption that FD is the only safe avenue for Investment - A lack of knowledge about different investment platforms usually leads to the belief that FD's are the only safe and profitable

avenues of investment.

- Debt trap keeps them under employment bondage with no freedom for major part of their productive life.

4

SEEDS OF POVERTY!

"No one comes to this world with a label of poverty. One should be smart enough to prevent others from attaching such a label."

- R Subramanya CFP

On the 12th of December, 2016, one of my mentees, Ganesh, asked me if I could help his friend and college mate, Anil, as he was under severe financial stress. I checked my schedule and scheduled a meeting the following week.

Ganesh had accompanied his friend, Anil, and introduced him to me and left immediately as he knew that I preferred discussing in private to maintain confidentiality.

I usually allow people to talk and express themselves as I can gather more information by listening than talking. Once they finish talking, I ask questions to get a complete picture and then analyze on how I can help them.

As Anil began to narrate his story, I gathered that he was from a middle class family. His father, in an unfortunate accident, had lost his right leg. Therefore his mother, a homemaker, had to shoulder the responsibility of the entire family. She was innocent and an introvert. But, life has ways and means of teaching and training people to move on. When his father was hospitalized after the accident, his mother had to go regularly to the hospital to take care of him. It was quite hectic as she not only had to take care of her children but also her husband. That's when she noticed many other women facing similar challenges.

On one such day, suddenly, she had an idea which eventually turned out to be her business. Like they say "Necessity is the mother of all Inventions". She started serving women and their needs. Although it was tough, she never gave up. Slowly her business picked up momentum and eventually took care of their family needs. Since they were a family of four, they were able to afford a decent lifestyle.

After completing Engineering, Anil was placed in an IT company with an annual pay of Rs.4,00,000. His family was thrilled.

Two months later, his neighbour, Janardhan, who was a money lender brainwashed Anil to purchase a two wheeler on loan at a nominal rate of interest. When Anil said that he had to confer with his parents, his neighbour also accompanied him. Janardhan, having planned this since the beginning, successfully convinced Anil's parents and soon Anil had a brand new bike.

Following this purchase, his expenses slowly started to rise. He had petrol expenses to take care of, took to the growing trends and bought new accessories for his bike and went on trips with his friends.

Six months later, Janardhan approached Anil's family again to sell them the idea of a personal loan for a bigger television and better furniture and they immediately signed up for it. They were all in high praise for Janardhan and his hassle-free money lending.

Soon, Anil's expenses increased further. Anil was starting to feel the pressure but the new channels on TV and the comfort of his new furniture numbed him to it.

Anil, went on to apply for credit cards and was elated by the power it had to offer. He convinced himself that he was independent and that he could always rely on his credit cards in times of emergencies.

Soon, Anil got married. His expenses only increased.

On the settlement of the bike loan, he decided that he wanted to purchase a car since most of his colleagues owned one. This time, he went straight to Janardhan and found his wishes fulfilled. By the time Anil could clear about 80% of his loans, Janardhan started seeding an idea of a dream house.

Two months later, Janardhan succeeded and Anil availed a housing loan from a nationalized bank where Janardhan was an agent. While Anil and his family were praising Janardhan for his timely help and resourcefulness, Janardhan was making plans for his own retirement.

Anil was falling into the rabbit hole of debt and life was slowly becoming miserable. He was constantly tense and was losing the love for his job. He began to blame his boss, company and colleagues for his misery.

When his college mates planned a trip, Anil spoke to Ganesh about how miserable his financial life was, which was when Ganesh reciprocated and described to him how he attained financial freedom in less than 10 years whilst being in his 9 to 5 job. A desperate Anil asked Ganesh for an introduction to his mentor at the earliest.

This is the back story of how Anil ended up in the seat in front of me.

It is truly upsetting to see youngsters being misguided by unscrupulous people for their own selfish motives and thereby push into a lifetime of suffering and slavery.

The next day, Ganesh arrived for our coaching session. He inquired if I was willing to aid his friend and I told him that I definitely would, considering I was a victim of something similar.

Ganesh is another client of mine. He was a 22 year old boy, from a middle class family, dependent on his mother's meagre income when he met me. With my guidance and support, he attained his financial freedom at 31. Anyway, I will discuss more about him in the upcoming chapters.

The following Tuesday, Anil had taken the day off from work, after scheduling an appointment with me. He came with all the records that he had. I wanted to understand all the mistakes that he had made.

I noticed that he was very good with excel. So, I gave him a template and asked him to fill in all information and reconstruct his financial life from day one. He sat in my office all day and put together information in the template and was waiting for me.

Later in the evening, I saw Anil sitting in the reception waiting for me. One look at him told me that he was firmly committed, just like Ganesh, and I was glad.

I went through his spreadsheet. I can't say it was 100% correct but I must say Anil did have an elephant's memory.

Following is the corrected spread sheet which Anil had created.

I will get back to Anil's financial life towards the end after I discuss the "Golden Rules" of money which were used to help Ganesh attain financial freedom within an unbelievably short period of 10 years, which every young and salaried person would love to have.

Table 1 – Anil's Financial Statement

Year	2000	2001	2002	2003	2004	2005	2006	2007	2008	2009	2010	2011	2012	2013	2014	2015	2016
Opening Balance	0	107214	186931	268836	324291	428136	-923062	-1297004	-1672487	-1924394	-2107629	-2300200	-2711379	-2825856	-2960875	-3136473	-3378284
Inflows-																	
Salary + Bonus	400000	440000	484000	532400	715640	858768	944645	1039109	1246931	1371624	1508787	1659665	2157565	2373321	2610654	2871719	3158891
Bank interest		4289	7477	10753													
Income from spouse																	
Total Inflows	**400000**	**444289**	**491477**	**543153**	**715640**	**858768**	**944645**	**1039109**	**1246931**	**1371624**	**1508787**	**1659665**	**2157565**	**2373321**	**2610654**	**2871719**	**3158891**
Outflows-																	
Living expenses	180000	198000	217800	239580	263538	289892	318881	350769	385846	424431	466874	513561	564917	621409	683550	751905	827095
Bike 60K	11786	23572	23572	11786													
Entertainment	48000	84000	102000	122400	146880	176256	211507	253809	304570	365484	438581	526298	631557	757869	909442	1091331	1309597
Clothing	12000	14400	17280	20736	24883	29860	35832	42998	51598	61917	74301	89161	106993	128392	154070	184884	221861
Education	18000	21600	25920	31104	37325	44790	53748	64497	77397	92876	111451	133742	160490	192588	231105	277326	332792
Insurance premium	23000	23000	23000	39000	46800	46800	46800	50700	50700	50700	50700	50700	50700	50700	50700	50700	50700
Car				23092	92369	92369	92369	92369	69277			197933	197933	197933	197933	197933	
Private loan interest							64000	64000	64000	64000	64000	64000	64000	64000	64000	64000	64000
Housing loan							495450	495450	495450	495450	495450	495450	495450	495450	495450	495450	495450
Marriage-self						1530000											
Total Outflows	**292786**	**364572**	**409572**	**487698**	**611795**	**2209966**	**1318587**	**1414593**	**1498838**	**1554859**	**1701357**	**2070845**	**2272041**	**2508341**	**2786251**	**3113530**	**3301495**
Closing Balance	**107214**	**186931**	**268836**	**324291**	**428136**	**-923062**	**-1297004**	**-1672487**	**-1924394**	**-2107629**	**-2300200**	**-2711379**	**-2825856**	**-2960875**	**-3136473**	**-3378284**	**-3520888**

1. INNER GAME OF MONEY

1a

SEEDS OF RICHES

"In times of change, the learners will inherit the earth."
- Bob Proctor.

Many years ago, on a Sunday evening, I was returning home with my wife after watching a movie. As we were nearing our house we saw a police vehicle near my friend's house. Two men in uniform were at their door talking to someone on the inside. We were worried as my friend had gone to Chennai on some official work.

We went over to check what was wrong. My friend's wife told us that the police were inquiring about their neighbors as there was a complaint against him. His name was Ramanan and he was a drunkard. Every day, he would come home drunk and create a racket by fighting with his wife. At least 5 houses on both sides could hear the screaming and crying every night. His wife, Padma, was a very nice lady. She was a school teacher. They had two school going children, a son and a daughter. Padma was a very responsible woman and the family was running on her earnings. Ramanan was nothing but a burden.

It appeared that that evening Ramanan was tormenting his wife for money so that he could go and get drunk. When Padma told that she had no money, her insane husband started to abuse and hit her. He dragged her out of the house and start to hit her in public hoping that she'd give him money to save herself from embarrassment. But Padma had had enough. She didn't budge. When her children came to her rescue, he kicked them mercilessly. One of the on-looking neighbors, unable to watch that cruelty any longer, called the police.

To everybody's shock and surprise, Padma and her brother went to the police station and somehow managed to get her husband back. Despite everything, to Padma, he was her husband.

Things appeared to be normal for a few days. But, old habits die hard. The screaming and shouting started again.

After a few days, Ramanan had gone to his village to attend a friend's wedding. Since they were all meeting after a really long time, they decided to have a drink together by the lake, just like old times. But, Ramanan drank one too many. One second they saw him standing with them. The next, he was being washed away by the water. Before anyone could come to their senses and realize what had happened, it was too late.

Padma and her children were traumatized and it took some time for them to come to terms with the tragedy. Although all Ramanan did was torture Padma, he was her husband and to lose him forever was too much for her to handle. With the help of close relatives and neighbors, they slowly started to regain confidence.

Padma slogged harder than before. She was more determined than ever to get her children educated. Her son Ganesh completed BE mechanical and got a job in a medium size firm with an annual pay package of Rs.3,70,000. When he got his first salary, he gave it to his mother and fell at her feet to thank her for everything she had done for him. He hugged her and promised to her that he would be a better man than his father ever was and the best son any mother could ever hope for. Padma's eyes welled up with tears. She was so proud of her son and was glad that all her hard work had paid off. Ganesh also told his mother that she could now rest at home and do whatever she loved and he would take care of the family.

He had only two goals. First, was to get his sister married and the second was to provide his mother with all the comforts she'd always dreamt of.

Padma distributed sweets to all her neighbors. When she came to give us sweets, we called her in. she was beaming. All she could talk about was how proud she was of her son.

Before leaving, she turned to me and said, "Sir, I have known you for so long and from what I've heard from other neighbors, you are a really good financial planner. Now that Ganesh has started to earn, I don't want him to spend it all and have nothing at the end of the month. So, if you could educate and guide him regarding his finances, it would be a big help."

Padma was a very diligent woman. Although she was a school teacher, she had realized how important it was to manage her money. I agreed to help her and her son without another thought.

Thus began Ganesh's financial journey with me. There are some who get into trouble and then maneuver their way out. And there are some others who take preventive steps rather than the detective. Ganesh belonged to the latter category. His life story can be a model for many youngsters. I have tried to cover his entire coaching in step by step sequence so that you can relate to it and also adopt these simple time-tested rules, templates, and techniques to attain financial freedom early in your life just like Ganesh.

In the world we live in today, people mismanage their income and don't fully understand the concept of borrowing. This, in turn, causes extreme havoc in every aspect of their life because, unfortunately, everything we do somehow in some way has a correlation to money.

Ganesh was from a south Indian Brahmin family. He was a very humble and charismatic person. He was such a warm person that he could make anyone feel comfortable around him. He obediently listened to his mother and followed my instructions. Every Sunday, he'd meet me from 7 to 8:30 in the morning and we'd discuss what had happened in the past week and what should be done in the next week.

1b

GOLDEN RULES OF MONEY

Note to readers:

This is a vast subject and we deal with this more in detail in our 3 days intensive workshop called "MGM" (Money Game Mastery), to train and equip participants to implement these proven and time-tested principles in their life so that they can reach their financial freedom faster, easier and in a most reliable way to have a life of their dreams.

My effort in writing this book is to sound a wakeup call to caution innocent youngsters to beware of their financial world and the next steps to proceed further.

I am really blessed to have had an opportunity to help thousands of people get the benefit of the sufferings of my life by guiding them with their finances. Every one of those who has taken financial education seriously has benefited tremendously and their testimonials speak for it.

I have been fortunate to have succeeded so far because I simply but strongly believe in leveraging. My simple strategy is to identify the pain points of an individual, his/her strong points and leverage one or many of those strong points to help them get out of debt trap to lead a life of their dreams.

Although the fundamental strategies are the same, the method may vary. It is like the principles of driving a car. One has to have the skill and experience to maneuver the vehicle depending on the situation and road conditions.

Here, in this book, I am discussing the principles that I have used with two of my clients to emphasize the need for financial education. But, this isn't the only strategy that can be used at all times as the strategies are tailor-made to suit the needs of individuals.

Hence, I am only touching upon the tip of the iceberg. However, readers are most welcome to contact me or my colleagues anytime for a better understanding of their financial health and how they can add meaning and direction to their financial world.

GOLDEN RULE 1

GRATITUDE IS THE WAY TO ABUNDANCE

"Attitude with gratitude determines your financial altitude"

- Shree Uday

On the first Sunday morning, at 7 am, Ganesh was seated opposite to me and was eagerly waiting for me to speak to him.

I took out my notebook, opened a page that I had marked specifically for beginners. "Read it out loud", I said.

"A grateful heart is a beginning of greatness. It is an expression of humility. It is a foundation for the development of such virtues as prayer, faith, courage, contentment, happiness, love and financial well-being."

He read it and looked at me. "Read it again. But this time,

place your right palm on your heart and as you enunciate each word, let it sink in", I said. He repeated this 3 times.

Not having completely understood, he looked at me with a questioning face waiting for me to go on.

I asked him, "Ganesh, what is it you just read?"

He said, "Sir, It is about being grateful."

I nodded and said, "You're right. This life is a gift from God. He has given us everything that we need for our entire life and we should be grateful for that. There are so many people, so many animals, and so many things around us which contribute to our wellbeing. As human beings, it is important that we recognize, appreciate and be grateful. The most important qualities any successful and wealthy person should have is generosity and gratefulness. When you are grateful for what you have, you start to appreciate its presence in your life. Consequently, you start to attract more of the same. This is how the Law of Attraction works."

An excerpt from the book "The Secret"- "Be grateful for what you have now. As you begin to think about all the things in your life you are grateful for, you will be amazed at the never-ending thoughts that come back to you of more things to be grateful for. You have to make a start and the law of attraction will receive those grateful thoughts and give you more like them."

I could see Ganesh nodding his head as he slowly started to comprehend what I was getting at. I gave him an agenda for the following week.

His first assignment was to maintain a journal of gratitude. The intention behind this journal was to note everything that he felt grateful for each day and to acknowledge and thank the source whenever he went through it again.

There are many known benefits of gratitude. It makes one feel more happy and content. When you feel grateful, you think of the all the things that you have. Not of the things that you don't. Therefore, you exude positive energy which eventually gets you all the things you want and need. It also makes us more likable and improves our health. Following are few scientifically proven benefits of being grateful.

- Gratitude increases your confidence.
- Gratitude helps you cultivate assertiveness.
- Gratitude helps you forgive and move on from the past.
- Gratitude strengthens your positive emotions.
- Gratitude removes your sense of entitlement.
- Gratitude improves your patience.
- Thankfulness allows you to let go of things that you cannot control.
- Gratitude helps you learn from your mistakes.
- Thankfulness helps you embrace change.
- Gratitude helps you practice self-love and self-compassion.
- Gratitude inspires you to use your time wisely.
- Gratitude makes you the master of your own happiness.

GOLDEN RULE 2

THE ONE IN THE MIRROR

"You are the creator of your own destiny"
- Swamy Vivekananda

The following Sunday, Ganesh was ready with a notebook and his journal. I looked at his journal. I saw that he had written about 100 lines. What caught my attention was the first line which read "I am truly grateful for my mother for everything that she has given me".

It showed that he was on the right track.

Then I asked him, "Ganesh, **tell me who is responsible for your life?"**

He responded, "My mother, Sir."

I asked him, "Are you sure?"

He was confused. I asked him again and he was unsure. I patted his back and said, "Don't complicate life by looking for difficult answers. In life, often, the most important things stem from simplicity."

I then narrated a story to him.

Priorities do change*

Once, in a forest, it rained heavily for few days. There was water everywhere. A monkey with its young one was stranded in a place which looked like an island due to rainwater. The monkey and its young one were perched on a tree and were hungry. The monkey could see a few trees with fruits a little away but it didn't know how to cross the flooded terrain.

It waited for few hours hoping that the water level would recede. When the water level dropped, the monkey held on to its young one and slowly climbed down the tree. Once on the ground, it cautiously stepped into the water and slowly started walking towards the trees that had fruits.

As it was crossing, the earth gave way and there was a sudden rush of water. The monkey began to panic as the water level started to rise at an alarming rate. As its survival instincts kicked in, it noticed a solid rock that could hold them for a while. It quickly jumped over and stood on the rock. Unfortunately, the water level kept rising and the monkey realized that its young one was in danger, so she kept rising the young one to keep it above water.

It so happened, that the water level rose to its face and finally covered its nose. Now the mother monkey realized that its life was in danger.

**The above story is to convey the meaning and I don't think any mother be it human or animal would sacrifice her own child.*

Not wasting any time, it lowered the baby monkey onto the rock and stood over it to save its own life.

This is life.

When it comes to one's survival, all else loses priority.

The smartness lies in carefully planning your life so that you don't encounter such situations.

After narrating the story, I asked Ganesh the same question.

"Who is responsible for your life?"

Now he was clear. He said, "I am responsible for my life, Sir."

I was happy that he was gaining clarity now. I told him to clearly define his life in words and come back after a week.

GOLDEN RULE 3

WHO ARE YOU RESPONSIBLE FOR

"We are made wise not by the recollection of our past, but by the responsibility for our future"

- George Bernard Shaw

Ganesh was, as usual, on time for the meeting. He was ready with his book on the table. Ongoing through his book, I knew for sure that he was committed to the path of financial education.

I asked Ganesh my second question.

"Ganesh, tell me, *who are you responsible for?*"

He was searching for an answer and to help him, I rephrased my question, "As an individual, in today's standing, who are you responsible for?"

He pondered for a while and said, "I am responsible for my mother and sister, Sir. I can't think of anyone else"

I asked him to think again.

He was trying to come up with an answer but without success.

I told him, "You, as an individual have many roles to play in life. But, as of today, you have one important role that is being a money generating asset. That is you are a money generating asset to yourself and your family. Keeping that as a pivotal role, tell me who are you responsible for?"

He was quick to tell me that he was responsible for himself and his family.

"Who else?" I asked.

He tried but couldn't.

Then I told him about "Farmer's theory."

Farmer's Theory

"Can you describe a farmer's life?" I asked.

Ganesh said that a farmer-led a very simple life. He works in the field, produces grains or other food supplements, keeps some for himself and sells the rest. Money thus made is used for his other requirements.

He was right, but partially.

Do you know why a farmer is happy and leads a peaceful life?

A farmer learns the art of living from his father, uncles and other senior farmers in the village.

Traditionally, a farmer's life was simple but, not anymore, due to urbanization, consumerism and cunning tactics of businessmen. As he grew, he picked up all good practices in the family. Earlier, farmers lived in big joint families. They had good value systems and respect for people, animals and Mother Nature in her entirety. Urban culture has killed all that.

Anyway, farmers had a simple, well defined "Responsibility circle" as shown in Figure 1. (We will discuss about Responsibility circle going forward)

Figure 1- Farmer's Responsibility Circle

Farmer's Responsibility Circle - RC

1. He would believe in God and grow foodstuff.
2. First 5% he would offer to God.
3. To maintain continuity he would preserve 15% towards the next crop.
4. Next 15% would be reserved for his cattle and other animals
5. Self-consumption 25%
6. 35% set aside for his future (Retirement plan)
7. 5% towards charity.

By having such a well-defined responsibility circle, he could lead a happy life.

I asked Ganesh if he understood what I was getting at. He nodded.

What I was teaching him was that he should create his own Responsibility Circle which he had not inherited from his father and he understood that. I advised him to create his own Circle.

He created his RC as follows.

1. Earn
2. Live
3. Family
4. Future
5. Charity
6. Friends and relatives

I asked Ganesh, "What is your aim in life?"

By now, he had understood me. And having seen me interacting with others and the kind of language that we generally use, he said, "Sir, I am committed to having both financial freedom and time freedom on my 40th birthday."

I asked him why he was looking for an early retirement.

He responded, "Sir, to start with, I know your story and I have heard a lot from you about the benefits of early retirement where one will have enough time and knowledge to help others live a happy life. I want to be a part of your mission. I don't want to see people failing in life the way my father did."

I was happy that not only did he not want to end up like his father but didn't want anyone else to either. I patted his back and said, "Ganesh, nothing comes easy, no pain no gain. For an Early retirement, you may face a lot of challenges, you may get discouraged and at times you may even feel like quitting. But once you get past that, the fruits of your struggle will be sweet. In the process, you may get tempted to cower back into your comfort zone. But, if you are determined to get out of your comfort zone you will reap the benefits of your hard work in the form of a spectacular life. Like J K Rowling once said "The only way out, is through."

So, are you ready?"

Ganesh was determined. He gritted his teeth and nodded his head. He said, "Sir, no matter what, I will not deviate from my path. Please guide me."

I smiled at him reassuringly and told him to spend quality time during the week to work on his responsibility circle and come prepared the following Sunday.

GOLDEN RULE 4

DEFINE YOUR OWN RESPONSIBILITY CIRCLE

"The price of freedom is responsibility"
- *Elbert Hubbard*

Following Sunday morning, Ganesh showed me his notebook where he had created his Responsibility Circle (RC) as follows.

Ganesh - Responsibility circle:

1. Family
2. Self
3. Future
4. Relatives
5. Friends
6. Charity
7. Society

After seeing his RC, I told him that I would like him to keep it simple and for that, I, metaphorically, divided him into 3 parts and assigned roles to each part.

I said, "Ganesh, listen carefully. You are going to play each part at a time and give it your all each time. Are you ready?"

Ganesh was all ears.

I then made the following diagram – Figure 2.

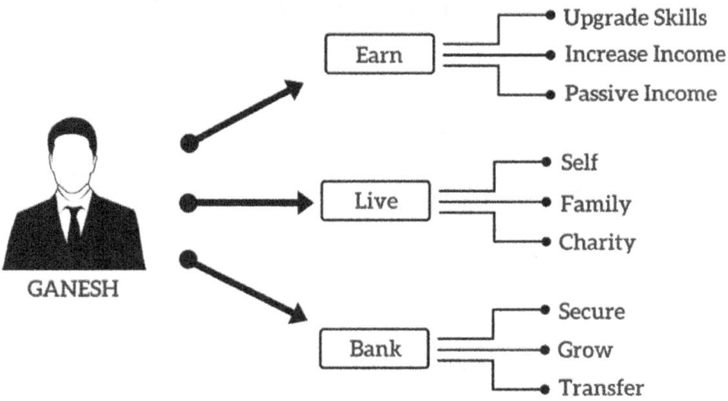

Figure 2 - Responsibility Circle

Your responsibility circle is as per Figure 2.

1. One part of you will focus on earning
2. Second part of you will enjoy life
3. The third part of you will be the banker.

He was trying to figure out what I had just drawn.

I went on, "Do you know why people are generally stressed and unhappy? Because they have forgotten the value systems given by their forefathers. They have fallen prey to a modern culture where everyone is trying to make money by using and manipulating others. I am not saying that one has to lead a rustic life like our fathers did. It's the thought process and the mindset that matters. They knew what they wanted and worked hard to get that. But in the contemporary world, more than one knows what he wants for himself, he is conditioned to believe and take to things he is being driven towards by his friends, society, and media.

The kind of advertisements that we see, the way the media works, everything is constantly bombarding us with ideas which make us believe sub-consciously that we need everything that is being advertised. That way, we end up buying them not knowing that our money is getting drained out faster than it comes in. We are constantly being driven towards consumerism not knowing its aftermath.

The most common problem with people is that they don't know where their money is going, how it is going and how to control it.

The urban theory is all about exploding consumerism in the minds of people and they would stop at nothing to achieve their objective. They have used two important tools to achieve their target, viz.

1. Break the joint family system that we were once proud of. This is done to divide one family into many families so that each family would buy more of the same.

2. Remodel education system to program and brainwash people into thinking that they are leading a spectacular life, but, in reality, are only leading a life of modern slavery.

It's time we understand the deception embedded in this so-called glamorous & modern culture and find our way back to our roots.

I concluded by asking Ganesh to review and come up with his strategies for the following Sunday.

ELB-Principle

The following Sunday morning, after having our morning coffee I began explaining, "You know, Ganesh, it took me years to understand what I am going to be explaining to you today. I am simplifying it for you by dividing it into 3 parts." He eagerly listened as I went on.

1. Earning Member:

As of now, you are qualified and ready to earn. So, some important points you should keep in mind are:

a. Upgrade Skills:

Do one thing at a time. When you play the role of an earning member, stay focused. Respect your job and never forget to thank your employer, your boss, your colleagues and all the others who are providing you with a platform to earn your livelihood. Constantly work on improving your skills and knowledge.

b. Increase Income:

On a day-by-day basis measure and improve yourself to become a highly effective and efficient person to earn more.

c. Passive Income:

Like Warren Buffet says, *"If you don't find a way to make money while you sleep, you will work until you die."*

What he is clearly telling us is that we should cultivate the habit of creating multiple sources of income which flow into our accounts without us being physically present. Since our work years are limited, work towards creating *permanent* passive income streams.

2. Living Member:

"Man is born to live, not to struggle".

You know that life is a gift from God and he has given equal opportunities to every individual. People fail to see this as they are kept in the dark by other selfish and more powerful people.

We should be smart enough to understand this and live our lives to the fullest.

How do we do that?

a. Self:

Like I told you we must live and experience our lives to the fullest. That is possible only when we learn to keep it simple and never let others force-fit their agenda directly or indirectly into our lives, by creating a budget to have complete control on our finances.

In the following pages we are discussing about Freedom Budget which has the potential to help one achieve financial independence faster.

b. Family:

As an individual, enjoy living a quality life. Keep life simple by not mixing it up with unnecessary things so that you don't have worries from the past carried to the future. Have a quality life with family, friends, people, and things that you are comfortable with. Don't bother about how money is going to come in as it has already been budgeted in your system.

c. **Charity:**

Be generous. Do charity. Help people who are in need. It not only helps them but also gives you an immense amount of satisfaction.

3. Banker:

This role of yours needs you to be a neutral person without emotions.

What do I mean by that? You should be a banker to yourself and your family within your RC. What is the main role of a banking system? Their main motto is to make profits out of the money they collect from others, keep their share of profits and give a pre-determined fixed amount to the depositors. Remember it is not a portion of profits but a pre-determined rate of interest.

You should acquire necessary skills and knowledge to do the following 3 things.

a. **Secure:**

You must protect all that you receive from the income. Care should be taken to see that it is safe and within reach. Remember, once the money comes to you (the banker), it should not go back to the first or the second person no matter what, because, it now belongs to your future.

(The importance of this will be covered in the following pages where I talk about "Lifeline")[1]

b. Grow:

Your main aim is to not keep that money idle. Every rupee should work every day, ie.24/7 and 365 days to grow in value. Here I want to stress upon one vital point- don't look at growing numbers but focus on growing value or enhancing your purchasing power. Never allow inflation to rob you of your future or your financial independence.

c. Transfer

Prepare and maintain proper documentation. Educate family members as per RC and be prepared to pass it on to the next generation with a WILL, Trust or other documents as may be necessary so that the next generation won't inherit misery in the form of confusion and court cases.

To summarize, I asked Ganesh if he was 100% clear on what he learned.

He nodded in agreement. I told him that many people find it weird when I say one should divide oneself into 3, 4 or 5 parts, as the case may be.

It is not physical division but an imaginary role that one must play to lead a spectacular life. Over the years, I have seen 100% success with people who have adopted this system of mine.

---

[1] *This is covered more in detail in our MGM 3 day's intensive workshop. For more details visit our website www.abundanceindia.com*

I told Ganesh to work on the same for next 3 weeks, create a monthly budget in consultation with his mother and sister and get them both for the next meeting on the fourth Sunday from then.

GOLDEN RULE 5

LITTLE MONEY VOICE

"Poverty or Prosperity takes birth in one's mind based on the seed planted by the early influencers"
- R Subramanya CFP

Ganesh was always on time. He was seated in my office with his mother and sister. After exchanging few pleasantries I stated the session.

I looked at Ganesh and told him “Ganesh, Imagine you're riding a two wheeler with your 5 year old son riding pillion. Your son sees many vehicles overtaking you and is puzzled and curious.”

“Dad, how is it that they are going so fast?”

“Why do you allow them to overtake us?”

“Why don’t you overtake all those vehicles?”

What would you do?

You would try to explain to him by saying that they are big and powerful vehicles with a higher capacity engine than your vehicle.

Being as reluctant as a kid, he’d ask you, “Then, why don’t you get a more powerful vehicle so that we can also go fast and overtake every vehicle on the road?"

You want to convince your son. So, you immediately stop the vehicle, get down and show your son the Speedo meter of your vehicle (Figure 3) and tell him that your Speedo meter has a limited range and it can only run to its rated speed.

Similarly every human has a mental money counter with different number of digits. To explain further, let me ask you a question.

Figure 3 – Speedo-meter

What is the maximum distance the meter on your vehicle can show?

You will count the number of digits as 5 and tell me that the meter can show a maximum reading as 99,999.

Now, my second question to you-what if you cover a distance more than 99,999 in a long period of usage?

You will surely tell me that once it crosses 99,999 km the meter will automatically reset itself to zero and start recording again.

This is exactly how our mental money counter works. Based on the number of digits in our heads, we earn. If it's 4 digits, we earn in thousands. If 6 digits, in lakhs and so on. The 4 digits can never become the 6 digits just like the odometer in the vehicle. Although the number of digits is limitless, people limit their capacity based on their LMV (Little Money Voice).

Now, let's say, you want a new computer. You discuss and finalize the kind of system you need and at what price you're willing to buy it.

Once the transaction is done, the computer dealer will unpack the system and install all the programs you need. After installation, he will demonstrate the functionality of the system.

Till the operating system & the software is installed, the system is like a newborn baby with an empty memory disc.

When a particular software is installed, it will produce the desired result related to that particular software. If a word is installed, it will produce results that word is expected to produce. If Excel is installed, it will function accordingly.

The question is, can you expect the word to perform the tasks that are programmed in Excel?

No, that is not possible. If you need a particular program you need that particular software. That means we are programming the new computer to behave the way we want it to; in line with our requirements.

Similarly, when you were born, you were also programmed on a day to day basis by your parents, friends, school, teachers, relatives, and society as per what they knew and believed. Eventually, they installed a master program called "your expectations" from this world for yourself. You then developed your own programs based on the knowledge and information received from all these sources. Some of the things etched in your mind maybe self-sabotaging but we don't realize that at the moment.

Imagine, you were born in a forest to poor tribal parents; they would have brought you up as themselves and you would have been a poor tribal.

Let's say, you were born to tribal parents and by a stroke of luck at birth, you were adopted by a rich American, Patrick.

What would be your identity today?

You would be a junior Patrick and wealthy.

This clearly shows that our life is purely dependent on the programs that go into our minds and not the environment, opportunities or the shortage of wealth in this world.

I call it, LMV – "Little Money Voice", which took birth the moment your brain started receiving information through what you saw, what you heard and what actions you took from then till today.

So, to be wealthy and successful you should systematically erase all the information in the brain cells that are programmed with LMV and methodically reprogram those cells with AMV[2] ("Abundant Money Voice") through Rapid programming (Figure 4) that we have developed after extensive research.

Figure 4 – AMV

[2]AMV – "Abundant Money Voice" is covered more in detail in our MGM 3 days Intensive workshop. Check our website www.abundanceindia.com for our next program.

The beauty is that, just by changing the program in your mind or your inner world, your outer world will automatically and permanently change.

Because we are living in a world of prosperity and nobody comes to this world with a label of poverty, it is people who program and push others into poverty and slavery.

We can get out of it, once and for all.

On explaining the concept of LMV to Ganesh, I told him to go down his memory lane and make a list of instructions related to money that he received from his parents based on their LMV.

His next task was to make a second list based on his own LMV that kept him in the dark and trapped his family in mediocrity.

Our next meeting was scheduled to happen three weeks from then.

GOLDEN RULE 6

AMV PARADIGM

"If you can see it in your mind;
you will have it in your hand".
-Bob Proctor

We were seated in my office and Ganesh had placed his book in front of me. Both sheets were filled with points. Since he knew of my preference for points that are short and crisp, he had filled it only with bullet points.

I glanced at them and was convinced that he had understood what was communicated to him.

Ganesh was eagerly waiting for me to speak to him and to confirm what he had recorded in his book.

I told Ganesh that he was on the right track. Then I went on to explain, "Anything in this world goes through 2 stages of manifestation."

1. Creative visualization
2. Materialistic manifestation.

Ganesh was curious. He asked me to explain.

I continued, "Whatever you want is created in your mind instantaneously and then again in reality. Imagine that your boss instructs you to prepare a presentation for his upcoming meeting. What do you do?

Without your knowledge or instructions, your mind will create an instant plan. It will analyze and create a strategy on its own even before you know what is happening. Then you will take control. You may assess the time that you have for the presentation and visualize a master plan, break it into small chunks and create a workable solution. All of this will happen in few seconds.

Then you will start taking action in the real world. The mind can create anything that you want in few seconds. But in the real world, it takes much more time."

They say that you reap what you sow, if you ideate what you need and take suitable actions, it will materialize.

If you want faster results, then the thoughts in your mind and your actions have to synchronize.

You, as an individual, will have your own aspirations in life. You may want to live in a big bungalow, drive the most expensive car and wear branded and world-class clothing etc.

What you need to do is to define all of your goals and to create a roadmap to reach those goals as per your time schedule. This will get done when both your inner world and outer world synchronize.

"Our Outer World is a mere reflection of inner world."

My experience with people is that when I ask them about their goals, they suddenly go blank. Their mind refuses to work. Why does this happen? Most people have no clarity and are very vague in life. They are so caught up in the day to day activities that they have no clarity on how they should plan and execute their goals. Their life is on some kind of a default mode which they have picked up from their parents or guardians.

During our MGM[3] workshop we show them their future in today's terms so that they learn to appreciate and take action.

The Figure 5 represents an average youngster's goal planning from the age of 22 when he starts earning on his own.

Once the goals are identified, we get them to work on the time schedule, amount required at the time of planning, resources available, responsibility, etc.

Further, we break them into small chunks of actionable steps to make it easy and simple.

The whole thing is documented and monitored on a regular basis and it is full of fun. People enjoy doing them.

[3] *This is covered more in detail in our MGM 3 day's intensive workshop. For more details visit our website www.abundanceindia.com*

We have already seen that our life is a reflection of our internal program called LMV. If we learn to reduce the influence of LMV slowly and steadily, it will vanish. As this is happening, we should also start programming our mind with a powerful program called AMV.

Once your aspirations and goals are aligned with your AMV, you will become unstoppable.

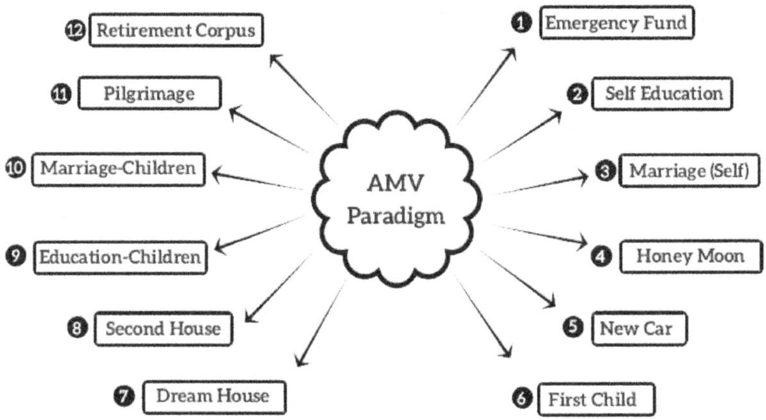

Figure 5 – AMV- Paradigm

I concluded the session by instructing Ganesh to prepare a list of his desires in the form of goals and come with a plan after 2 weeks.

GOLDEN RULE 7

FINANCIAL BASE

"Always stay grounded by connecting to the roots"
-R Subramanya CFP

Ganesh was well prepared for our next meeting. He showed me his cash flow tracker and the list of goals. Everything seemed to be in order. I was really glad seeing him make great progress.

I started by telling Ganesh that it takes about 22 years for an individual to get educated and qualify himself to earn his living. But if one gives it a thought, it mustn't take us that long. The reason is that our education system is not holistic.

It teaches us a particular syllabus which is predetermined by an official body. This syllabus is not based on one's personal aptitude, likes and dislikes. Therefore, even after graduation, half of them are still clueless about what they want to do. Study Certificates have become more of a safety net. If what they want to do doesn't pan out, they cower back to their qualifications.

Our education system does not make us life-ready, i.e, there is no practical training as to how an individual can acquire skills and techniques to understand his passion and choose the right direction.

22 years of your life you were being trained for only one thing - to become a money generating asset. We were all sent to schools and colleges. But, despite all that, we all end up becoming a slave – a slave to our money.

Ganesh was really quiet. He was processing the new information he'd been bombarded with. "That's a perspective I never considered, Sir." I gave him some time to comprehend and analyse.

Then I went on.

If one joins armed forces, say army, what do they do? Irrespective of where you are from, your background, your culture, they will take you through both theoretical and practical training till you attain the necessary skills and techniques that are expected of a soldier.

Similarly, a doctor or a CA has to work under the guidance of seniors before he can be on his own.

But for the most important aspect in our lives, our financial life, where is the training? Which school or college is imparting that knowledge to us?

Financial education is crucial for us to be able to make a decent living.

Another thought provoking question for Ganesh to ponder over. He sat down and thought. "This is starting to make so much sense, Sir."

"Your assignment for the next week is to identify five situations in life where one can survive without money."

With that, we concluded the meeting.

GOLDEN RULE 8

FINANCIAL LIFE > PHYSICAL LIFE

"Man is born to live. Not to prepare for life"
-Boris Pasternak

The next Sunday, I was very eager to meet Ganesh as I wanted to know if he'd found an answer to my question. I asked him and he said, "Sir, it seemed like such a simple question but the moment I sat down to pen it down, I couldn't find even a single situation unless one is ready to live in the forest."

I smiled. I took his book and made the following sketch.

1. Physical life!

The average life expectancy of the average Indian is 77 years (Figure – 6).

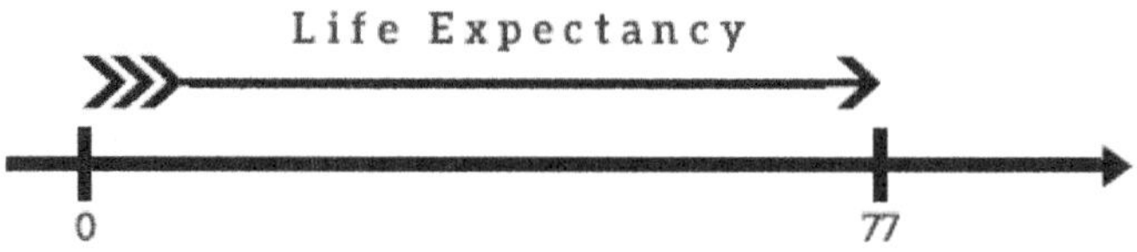

Figure 6 – Life Expectancy

In the next 30 years, it is likely to touch 100 years.

Ganesh looked surprised.

I asked Ganesh what he thought was the average life expectancy of an Indian before independence. He believed it to be over 100 years.

I corrected him and said that the average Indian, before attaining independence, lived up to about 45 years. Although a few people survived for a long period, the majority of people perished due to epidemics, lack of hygiene and sanitation and various other issues that we, fortunately, don't face today.

Let's assume that, for all practical purposes, we consider physical life to be from 0 to 100 years as per Figure 7.

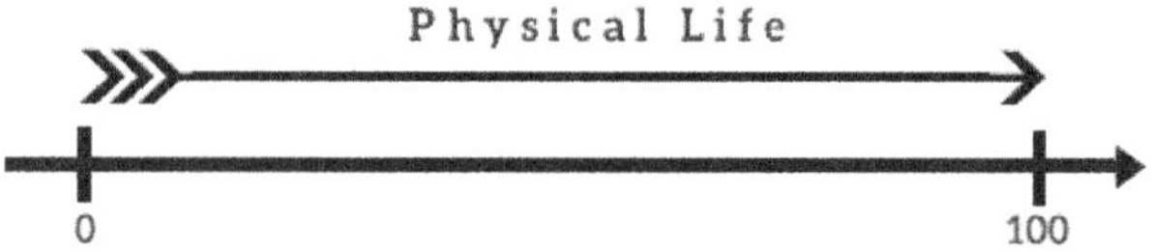

Figure 7 - Physical Life

2. Productive life!

"Ganesh, on an average, how many years is one productive?

He gave me a rough figure of 30 years.

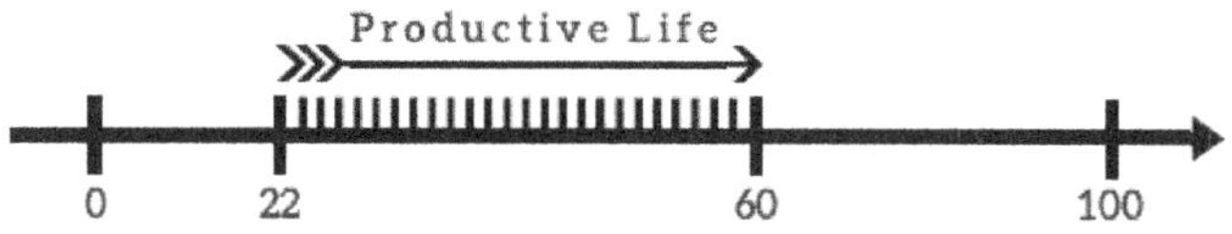

Figure 8 - Productive Life

I nodded and explained, "Every individual has 3 stages in life namely education, productive life and retired life. Of these, productive life as per Figure 8 derives its strength from financial education which plays a very important role and determines how enjoyable your retired life will be.

One's productive life usually starts somewhere around 22 years and goes on till 60 years of age i.e., 38 years of productive life.

The income that one generates during his productive life should not only take care of him and his dependents during this period but also his entire retired life.

3. Financial life!

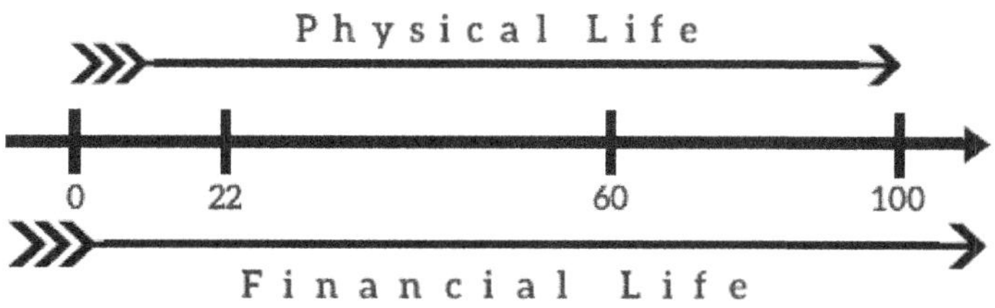

Figure 9 – Financial Life

I then asked Ganesh. "Ganesh, tell me when the need for money starts in one's life and when does it end?"

He looked at me and said, "Sir, it will start at birth and end at death."

Smiling at the generic answer, I said, "As per Figure 9 need for money starts even before a person is born and continues even after he dies.

When a couple is expecting a baby, the mother has to visit the doctor on a regular basis, consume nutritious food and take care of her own health. All of this costs money. Therefore, expenses are incurred even before one is born. Also, we as Indians, have certain duties to uphold on the death of a family member. Some of the rituals are to be performed year on year while some others are to be done only once. Either way, it's certain that money is required even after one's death.

Ganesh nodded comprehendingly.

I went on. "Isn't it odd that although our life span is from 0 to 100, money requirement extends beyond both the limits?"

Again, he nodded expecting me to continue.

"There are myriad creatures walking on the face of earth. Life cycle of all of it is the same – Take birth, thrive and survive, die - No different from humans. God bestowed humans with thinking capacity and differentiated us from the rest. But, humans found another way – Money. No other creature in this world requires money other than humans."

I paused.

"Whatever we need for today, tomorrow and the rest of our lives has already been created by God. Not just for humans but for every creature that can breathe.

Despite everything available in such abundance, we suffer throughout and constantly run after money. Why?"

Ganesh tried to find an answer. Not being able to, he looked at me. I continued.

"In the name of civilisation, man has brought in a barrier called money between him and everything else in this world. Money came into existence as a convenient means of exchange for goods and services. But now, it has become a privilege in the hands of the rich and mighty.

Of late, it has become a huge and complex system beyond the control of individuals. Money is indispensable as it plays a crucial role in all our lives. So, the smarter approach would be to understand the system and use it to our benefit instead of cribbing about how miserable it is."

I told Ganesh to meet me second Sunday from then to continue on the same golden rule.

4. Money habits

Sunday morning, at 7 am, Ganesh was seated opposite to me and was eagerly waiting for me to continue.

I began explaining.

For years, I have been analysing salaried people and their money habits. From my observations, I noticed that the majority of them had a particular way of handling their money. To understand this better refer Table 2 let us say a person works for the month of January. He gets his salary and that takes care of his financial requirements for the month of February.

Now, imagine he doesn't work during February due to illness; company lay off, accident or any such reason. Then he won't be receiving any salary for the month of February.

I looked at Ganesh and asked him, "What do you think will happen?"

Ganesh said that he would use his savings and if he hasn't got any, he'd borrow from friends and relatives.

I agreed. "But what if his income stopped for a few months or years?" I probed.

January	→	Salary	→	February
February	→	X	→	???
March	→	X	→	???
April	→	X	→	???
May	→	X	→	???

Table 2 – Salary Dependency

Ganesh's face became more serious. He imagined such a situation for a while and finally said, "it'll start to get really difficult, Sir. He will have no money. To survive, he'll borrow more and more obvious to the fact that he's only digging his grave deeper. "

I nodded and asked, "Don't you think such a situation will arrive in every individual's life on the day he retires?"

This question hit Ganesh hard. "I have never given that a thought, Sir. Now that you put it this way, it's starting to make a lot of sense."

I took that as my cue and went on.

5. Retired life!

I asked Ganesh what he thought retired life was.

Ganesh said, "Sir, it is when a person stops working after he reaches a certain age, stipulated by his employer."

"You are telling me what retirement means. I am asking you what retired life means." I said. Looking at Ganesh clueless, I said, "Retired life is the number of years after one's retirement until the end of his life." Refer Figure 10.

Figure 10 – Retired Life

"We have already established that our financial life is longer than our physical life, that is, money is required at every stage of life, before, and after. We have also seen that whatever a person generates during his productive years gets consumed to cater to his immediate needs thereby leaving behind a very meagre savings. If this is the regular pattern, how can one survive after retirement?" I asked rhetorically.

I took Ganesh's silence as my cue and went on. Earlier, the joint family culture protected senior members of the family till the end. But, given to urbanisation, joint families are hardly found anymore.

Generally, a healthy person would retire at 60.

Post this, his active income will automatically stop for obvious reasons. So, given this, how does one hope to survive after retirement? Should one think about this on the day he retires or today, at the very moment?

"Today, Sir. At this very moment." Ganesh said nodding his head.

I further explained, "One has to plan one's finances at the earliest. The best time to plan finances was yesterday and the worst time, tomorrow. So, now that yesterday is gone, what is left? Today and right now."

TRICKLING SEEDS

"Stop consuming seeds,
Learn to convert them into fruits first".
- R Subramanya CFP

I have said this before but I will reiterate - We live in a world that provides us everything in plenty. Nature has everything that we need and more for today, tomorrow and the rest of our lives.

Despite this, why is it that only some people are rich and wealthy while the others lead a life of hard work and financial stress?

When all the riches are already available in this world, when everyone has equal time and opportunities, the irony is that the top 1% of the world owns more than half of world's wealth while the rest lead a mediocre and troubled life.

After explaining all this, I asked Ganesh, "why is it so?"

Ganesh shrugged his shoulder and I went on, "One may have great knowledge and skills but if his LMV (Little Money

Voice) is not converted to AMV (Abundant Money Voice) to synchronize with his outer reality (desires), there is no way he can get rich and wealthy. It is as simple as that.

To explain further, let me give you an analogy.

Consider 4 people standing on the sea shore. One with a cup, the second with a bucket, the third with a tanker and the fourth has come to build a pipeline. The source is the same for each of them, but what they take is what they think they can.

Similarly, wealth is available in plenty in this world, what we take is based on our inner belief system i.e. LMV or AMV. One earns only as much he believes he can. Therefore, it is clear that one's inner belief, his Little Money Voice (LMV) can only guarantee a mediocre life and nothing beyond.

How to get wealthy?

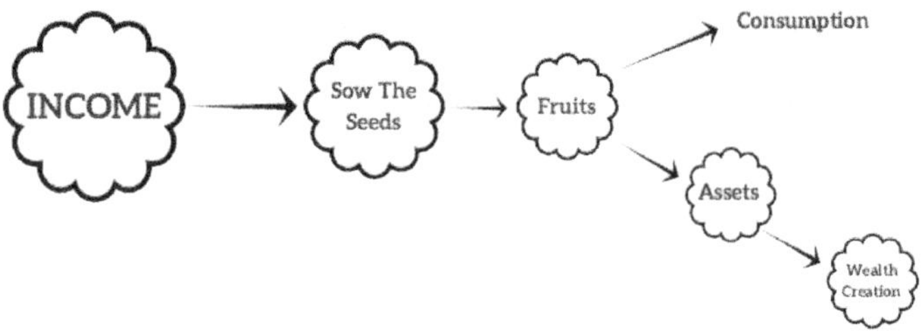

Figure 11 –Principle of Wealth

The fundamental principle of wealth creation is as per (Figure 11).

If you are merely investing your time, physically and mentally, to earn a livelihood, you'd earn just seeds. To cater to your immediate needs, you will end up consuming them thereby leaving you with nothing for the future.

But, instead of consuming the seeds at its rudimentary stage, if you sow the seed and consume its fruits, you will have enough to cater to your present needs and to plant more for your future.

This is what I call the "*Farmer's theory*".

If you consume a seed, it is gone forever. But, on the other hand, if you convert it into fruits, a single seed can produce countless number of fruits in the long run. On similar lines, if you consume all your income for your immediate needs, you'd be left with nothing for the future. Therefore, individuals must use a part of their income to create passive income streams which will work for them even when they aren't working.

This is a very vital principle[4] of wealth creation.

He nodded his head slowly taking in all that I had just said.

I concluded our meeting telling Ganesh to get back after 2 weeks.

---

[4] *This is covered more in detail in our MGM 3 day's intensive workshop. For more details visit our website www.abundanceindia.com*

GOLDEN RULE 9

5 D'S OF LIFE

"Life is not a problem to be solved,
But a reality to be experienced".
- Soren Kierkegaard

I asked Ganesh, "Do you know the 5 D's of Life?"

He shook his head.

"Every individual is subject to experience the following aspects in his life time."

1. Desires

We all have desires. Though our desires may change from time to time, it will continue up to the end of one's life. The extent of which, may, however, vary from person to person. To fulfil one's desires, money is essential.

2. Disease

Disease is a part of one's life. Day by day, new diseases are being discovered that cost a lot of money to treat. One has to be prepared at all times.

3. Disability

Disability may be physical, mental or psychological but it causes turbulence in one's life regardless. One has no choice but to be prepared financially to deal with it.

4. Disaster

Natural calamities, accidents, loss of loved ones, loss of job/money or other unforeseen situations can disturb anybody.

Financial preparations are a must to be able to handle such a disruption in life.

5. Death

Death can cause a major imbalance in a person's life. If the bread winner is lost, then the family will face hardship if they are not prepared financially.

We quickly wrapped up telling Ganesh to meet me the following Sunday as I had other engagements.

GOLDEN RULE 10

STATUS-QUO

"When your self-worth goes up,
your Net-worth goes up with it"
- Mark Victor Hansen

Ganesh and family were present and were as enthusiastic as ever.

As I settled down, his mother told me that they were fortunate to have gotten an opportunity to learn valuable lesions on money.

I thanked her for her kind words and began my session.

"Ganesh, we all have aspirations. We all want to be happy and wealthy. But, we don't know how. Our upbringing and schooling has only given us half the knowledge and skills required to live a life of our dreams. For a tree to have a strong trunk, its roots must be stronger. Similarly, if you wish to grow rich, you must first understand the strength of your foundation (Status-quo).

Ganesh leaned forward and listened as I explained about what net worth is and how one can augment it.

Net Worth

The first step in achieving any goal is by knowing two things –

- Where are you currently?
- Where you wish to go?

On parallel lines, In the financial world, for one to achieve any goal, he must know his Net worth. Net worth is the difference between your assets and liabilities. Liabilities indicate how deep are you? from ground zero and your assets indicate how high are you from ground zero.

Assets – Liabilities = Net Worth

It is a simple indicator yet a very powerful tool for decision making. "Generally most individuals ignore this and if asked about what their net worth is they are clueless. This is not a good sign because people don't know where they are and what is even worse; they don't know where they want to go."

I asked Ganesh. "Ganesh, do you know your net worth as of now?"

He was happy that I asked him that question. He opened his book and showed me the following Table 3.

I was happy that he was learning fast.

Sl.No.	Description	Asset	Liabilities	Net-worth
1	Cash	8,600		
2	Savings acc.	34,000		
3	Bank FD	50,000		
4	Education loan		72,000	
	Total	92,600	72,000	20,600

Table 3 – Net-worth of Ganesh

I asked Ganesh, "Ganesh, are you happy with your current situation?"

He said. "Sir, I am happy that I am not below ground zero but, not too happy as I am just above ground zero."

I reassured him that he is on the right path and it is now a question of time.

I concluded our meeting by telling Ganesh and family that the following week was going to be more important as I was planning to work on their cash flow and they should come with details of their cash outflows.

GOLDEN RULE 11

CASH FLOW PUZZLE

"Cash is Prince, Cash Flow is King and Investment is the kingdom".
– R Subramanya CFP

As usual, Ganesh entered my office at 7 in the morning. After some discussion about how the previous week went, I told him about the day's agenda – Cash flow management.

I began, "Cash flow management is the blood line of any individual or family. Some consider it to be trivial while some are scared of the reality it might unfold.

Cash flow analysis may be embarrassing to those who are always short of cash due to over spending. But on taking a closer look, one may find ways and means to cut down on extra expenses. Hence, regular cash flow management and reviews are integral parts of one's financial wellbeing.

Imagine, your regular electricity consumption is 500 units per month. All of a sudden, Electricity board brings in a regulation saying that you can only use 300 units per month and once it reaches that limit, the supply will automatically be disconnected and a fresh quota of 300 units will be allotted on the 1st of the following month putting you into darkness for the rest of the month.

What would you do?

Ganesh said, "Sir, we will take all necessary precautions to make sure that we will keep our consumption within that limit.

I said, "Good. But, you are used to consume 500 units per month. How will you manage within 300 units?"

Ganesh said, "Sir, we will plan and monitor to keep it under the limit."

I nodded and said, "Good. So, tell me, when will you plan?"

Ganesh said, "At the beginning of the month, Sir."

I shook my head lightly and said, "No, Ganesh. You need to plan even before the month has begun."

To explain why I had given him such a scenario, I said, "General tendency of people is that they don't bother unless there is some stronger regulation.

Let's say electricity board sends its staff door to door and asks them to make announcements to inform people to reduce their electricity consumption. Do you think it will have any effect at all? No, unless there is a regulation to punish or penalise, people will pay no heed."

When it comes to money, people, especially, young and salaried category get swayed by false prestige and to please others spend not only what they earn but more than what they earn. This is because since childhood, people always said – "Earn so that you can spend". Therefore, people are programmed to spend whatever they earn. They are impulsive and spend without thinking about its repercussions.

When I was a boy, while playing with stones and sand, I saw my mother write something. I went and sat next to her to see what she was writing. Back then it didn't make much sense. But as I grew, I understood how important it was. She was making a family budget on the red-oxide flooring with a soft stone to write. My father had given her some money; she was deciding what expenses she'd be incurring. Despite not having had any education, she had enough knowledge to know that she had to have control over money or she wouldn't be able to feed so many mouths.

What I learnt from that experience is that we need to decide where our money is going beforehand so that we control money instead of money controlling us. Trial and error does not work with money as earning money is not as easy as losing it.

Hence, having a cash flow system to suit your requirement based on your responsibility circle is very critical not only to have a financially stress free life but also to attain your financial freedom at the earliest.

I then showed 2 cash flow templates to Ganesh.

- Macro template
- Micro template.

I told Ganesh that he has to fill information in both the templates. But asked him to fill the Micro template first so that the Macro template could be filled in the next week.

He looked at me and was about to ask me why not both the templates. Sensing that, I told Ganesh not to bother about it for now as he would get his answers in the following meeting.

Meeting was thus concluded.

Ganesh and family were seated in front of me the following Sunday.

He showed me the template.

I went through it and found it exhaustive but not clear.

"Good job. Now, let's fill in the Macro template as per your RC (Responsibility Circle)."

As Ganesh was busy summarising inflows and out flows, his mother asked me how to plan for their daughter's education and wedding expenses of both her children. I assured her that it was already taken care of and she needn't worry about it.

Ganesh finally showed me the template and after discussing with them it was finalised (Table 4).

Sl. No.	Description	Inflow	Outflow	Surplus
1	Salary	3,70,000		
2	Bank Interest	344		
3	Family deity		3,700	
4	Charity		3,700	
5	Living Expense		74,000	
6	Entertainment		14,800	
7	Clothing		7,400	
8	Education		7,400	
9	Pilgrimage		20,000	
	Total	**3,70,344**	**1,31,000**	**2,39,344**

Table 4 – Cash flow Surplus

I then went on to explain to his mother that the key to financial well-being is having a positive surplus at all times.

She was not clear.

Then I told her that a positive cash flow is

Income – Expense = Surplus.

If surplus is positive, their cash flow is positive else it indicates trouble. The simple rule is to follow the RC and make sure that your surplus is always positive.

I told her that over a long period of experience I have created a simple thumb rule - a 3 step action plan.

1. Categorise expenses as per your RC
2. Fix a percentage of your income for each category
3. Invest the surplus without delay.

Ganesh asked me, "But, why the percentage, Sir?"

I told him that fixing a percentage of your income is the simplest and easiest way to have total control over your finances. If income goes up proportionately expenses also go up and so does your surplus and vice versa.

Once you fix the percentage, it can work for a long time without drawing your attention month on month.

They nodded in agreement and the meeting was sealed for the day.

GOLDEN RULE 12

AERIAL VIEW

"Mediocre life is the result of worm's eye view. Financial success is the outcome of bird's eye view of your financial life"

- R Subramanya CFP

I was surprised to find only Ganesh sitting in my office. I asked him if we can start or wait for his family.

He asked me to go on as they weren't expected.

I began. Ganesh, "Imagine you are in a game of maze. You enter and keep moving based on the guidance given by your mind. What might happen? You may keep moving in different directions but you may not find your way out. Even if you want to trace back to your starting point and get out of the maze, you may fail. You may get disappointed and frustrated but that won't help you find your way either. But imagine, if you had wings, you could've flown up, and studied the entire maze and found your way out.

Sometime during 2002, I had gone on a tour to a place called Khanapur in Belgaum district. We were a group of 6 friends. David, the owner of the resort where we had planned to stay, came to pick us up. He was originally from Goa and had a nice resort about 15 km inside the forest. His wife helped him manage the resort.

David had a modified Jeep that looked pretty bad but had a powerful engine and high chassis to run on rough terrain. Both David and his jeep did an excellent job in transporting us to different places.

We had planned to stay there for 5 days. On day 4, we went to visit breath-taking waterfalls called Vajrapoha. Since it was inside the forest, not many go there as it is extremely dangerous and without a local guide it is impossible to go and return in one piece.

David knew the place well and he was equipped with a compass, a powerful binoculars & GPS device. First, we drove into the forest for about 15 kms. Parked the jeep there and started walking.

After about an hour of walking, we saw a stream brimming with fresh water. David said, "If anyone wishes to take a quick dip, you can." It was such a lovely place that all of us jumped in even before David could complete his sentence. David showed us how to choose a safe spot in the stream and we thoroughly enjoyed ourselves.

The flow of water was good. Along the stream, there were 2 small rocks with a narrow gap. Since the width suddenly decreased here, the force of the water was massive. David, being a localite, swam and sat under the tiny waterfall. Seeing him, I was tempted as well. I sat there and it felt like my entire body was being massaged. It felt absolutely amazing. Each of us took turns to sit there. After a while, David signalled that it was getting late and we had to move on. Unable to leave the place just yet, I went and sat there again. David called again, I didn't pay heed. It was so refreshing that I lost track of time.

The next time I open my eyes, I see that all my friends have already gone. I dashed to the bank, changed my clothes and ran. After about 2 furlongs, the path was dividing itself into two. I looked at both. Seeing that the path on the right seemed wider, I assumed that that would be the road they'd taken.

I walked for about 5 minutes. The jungle was getting thicker and thicker and I couldn't find my group. I started to panic. I had lost my direction. I didn't know where I was or how to get to them.

I quickly turned back and started running towards the junction from where I had turned right. This time, I took the other road. I ran as fast as I could. I ran for about 1 km and still found no one. Now, I was really scared. I had read about how trekkers lost their way in the forest and were never found. I didn't want to be one of those trekkers. Wherever I turned, it all looked the same. It was so similar that if I turned 360 degrees, I wouldn't know in which direction I had first started.

I didn't know what to do. Suddenly I had an idea. I looked around and found a tall tree which I could climb. Not wasting another minute, I started to climb. I climbed about 20 feet and I looked around. I could see only trees all around. I climbed higher and higher. My heart was thumping. I was about 40 feet above the ground. I looked around again. I could see a plateau a little away from where I was. I kept staring in the direction of the plateau.

Suddenly I saw a black thing moving. I kept staring at it. After few seconds I saw more of them and realized that they were my friends.

I quickly got down and started running in that direction.

After running for about 30 minutes, I found them. I shouted at the top of voice to make them stop. All of them turned at once. I was so furious at David at how irresponsible he was for not noticing that I wasn't even there. David smiled and said that I deserved it and continued walking. I was shocked at his audacity.

After about 5 minutes, he looked at me and said, "The jungle is a dangerous place and one cannot take things for granted here. I clearly asked you to get dressed and leave. You aren't the first to not pay heed. Initially, when people used to not listen, I used to get all worked up. But, now, I carry on and they learn a lesson by themselves. I was shocked. "What if I hadn't found my way? What if I had gotten lost in the jungle? What good will your lesson do if I'm dead?" I said, all in one breath. I just couldn't digest the fact that he'd left me behind deliberately.

He smiled at me and then made a strange noise. All of a sudden, out of nowhere, a man holding a long stick appeared before us. David spoke to that man in a language which none of us could understand. After a brief conversation, that man disappeared.

Then David told me, "That man you saw was always tailing you all this while you didn't even know about it. He just told me about what all you did up there." Everyone burst out. Having gotten out of that situation, I found it funny too. But, what I learn that day in the forest was etched in my memory forever."

I then asked Ganesh. "Why do you think I'm telling you this story here?"

I took his silence as my cue and went on.

Having been stranded in an unknown land, I was petrified. I saw no way out from where I stood. I had to do something and had to do it fast because, with every passing second, my friends were going farther away. Therefore, I started to run and save time.

Realising that my actions weren't getting me to where I want to go, I had to find a more effective way. Therefore, I climbed up a tree to get an aerial view of the terrain so that the range of my vision would increase.

This is how our life works too. In our day to day life and, especially, our financial life, we only have a surface view which has limitations. We don't have enough data to make informed decisions and hence, end up making mistakes.

Therefore, in order to avoid this, we should be in a position to have an aerial view of our financial life. Better still, a mentor or a coach like David in my story can create an aerial view of our life and guide us with the right strategies.

Figure 12 is an aerial view of a sample Financial life. It is easy to create, easy to understand, easy to modify, easy to implement and easy to monitor.

When I showed him this sample aerial view, Ganesh looked at it trying to absorb as much as he could. I allowed him to grasp whatever he could. After 2 minutes he thanked me profusely for sharing valuable inputs with him.

He said. "Sir, I am the luckiest as I am getting so much value at an early stage of my life. I whole heartedly thank you and God for all your support.

I was feeling great that I was able to add value to his life.

We closed our meeting with an understanding that we would be meeting on the following Sunday for another important session.

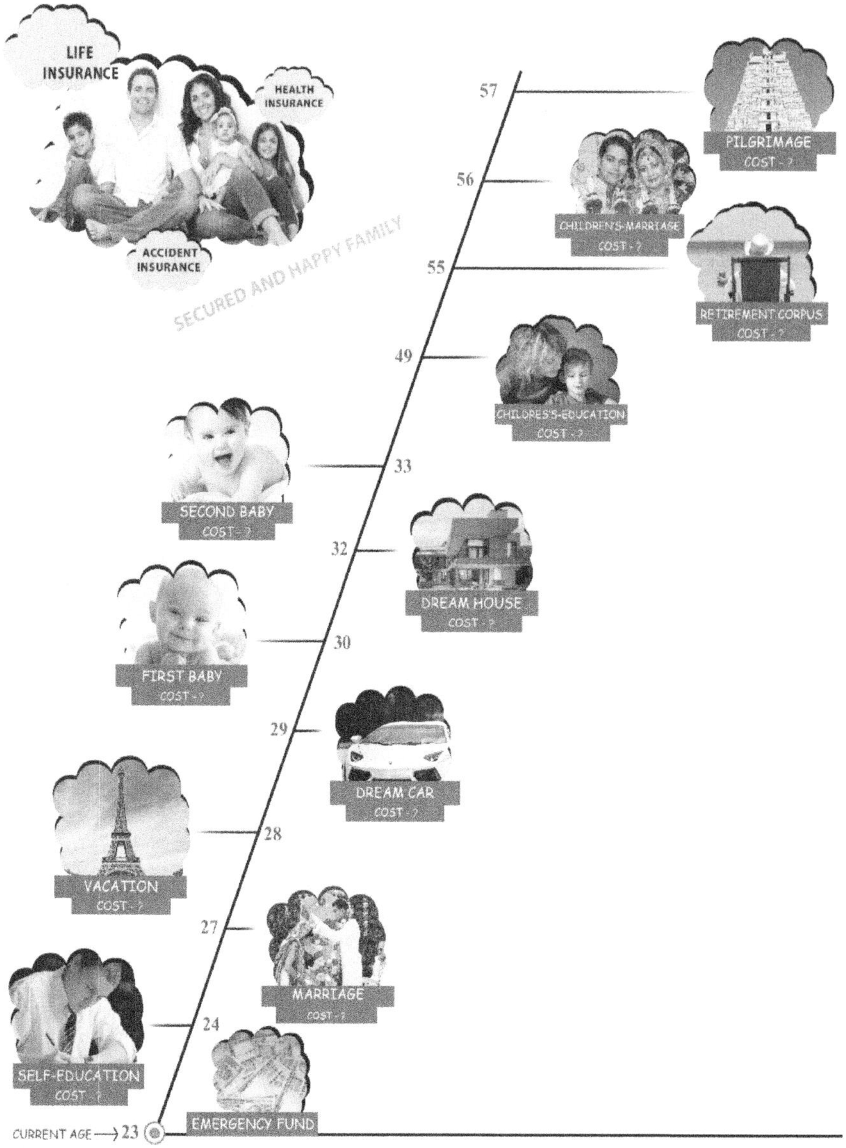

Figure 12 – Financial Aerial View

GOLDEN RULE 13

GAME CHANGER - BUDGET

"A budget is telling your money where to go instead of wondering where it went".

-Dave Ramsey

This week, I had asked Ganesh to get his mother along as we were going to discuss about budgets and budgets work only with the cooperation of the entire family.

Ganesh showed me budget he had created with his mother's help.

I was happy with how they had documented every small expense. It showed me that they had sat and discussed at length and prepared this.

I then grouped all their expenses into 3 categories as below and said, "Now that they are grouped, you will have better control."

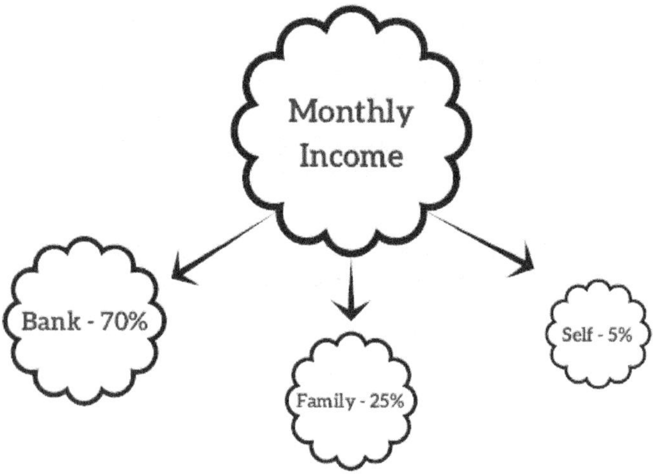

Figure 13 – Freedom Budget

Considering the data from the budget, I did some math and allocated a percentage of their income to each group and asked Ganesh if it was feasible.

He said, "Yes, sir."

But I asked him to think for a bit because when one is preparing a budget, on seeing how much expenditure he is incurring, he'd try to cut corners and show a smaller figure to make himself feel better. So, I asked Ganesh again, "Is this a practically workable budget?"

He gave it another thought and said, "Yes, Sir. This will work."

After a pause, he added, "My mother wants to help me by giving me her income as well, Sir, as she thinks I am being overburdened. But I wish to handle this by myself."

I smiled and looked at Padma and said, "Your son is a very challenging boy. He's been doing really great since the start and I can assure you that that he will ace this as well."

My words comforted her and she agreed to let Ganesh handle it by himself.

I then explained to them about what the preconceived notions about a budget and how a budget affects one's life.

"You know why most people are scared of the word 'budget'?" I asked.

Ganesh shrugged his shoulders. I went on, "Because they fear that they may be doing it wrong and unfortunately, since most people are clueless about their money, they end up doing it wrong. So, when it doesn't work out as planned the first time, they completely abandon the thought of budgets which only worsens the situation. You see how it becomes a chain reaction?"

Ganesh nodded.

"Generally, for most money comes in sparingly and vanishes even before they can feel it in their hands. Budgeting tends to show them this harsh reality and the magnitude of underlying problems. So, people avoid the fear or embarrassment by not creating a budget at all. But, What they fail to understand is that they are only pushing and accumulating their problems into something more catastrophic."

"Therefore, I first clear off this preconceived notion in my clients' mind before asking them to prepare a budget. Budget is just a tool that we use to get a bird's eye view of our money management so that we can take an informed decision on how to change it to suit our requirements."

They both nodded.

"Creating a budget is hard. But adhering to the prepared budget is harder. Therefore, you must commit to each other that you will not deviate from the budget at any cost."

"Yes, Sir", they said unanimously.

I then shared a template with Ganesh to track their day to day expenses and monitor that with reference to their budgeted values.

Our next meeting was scheduled 4 weeks later.

GOLDEN RULE 14

ELIGIBILITY INDEX - EI

"Do not save what is left after spending, but spend what is left after saving"
- Warren Buffet

Ganesh, "Imagine I tell you to lift an object that weighs 5 kg.

What would you do?"

He said, "I will lift it".

I asked, "if I ask you to lift a 50 kg load. Would you lift it?"

He agreed.

My next question was, "in case I tell you to lift a 200 kg

load. What will you do?"

He responded, "Sir, I would humbly refuse as it is not practically possible for me."

I continued, "Imagine that I get a world class coach to train you in weightlifting and he teaches you every technique that there is, for about 2 years. You become a champion. Then, if I ask you to lift a 200 kg load, would you still refuse?"

Ganesh enthusiastically said he wouldn't refuse.

I further explained that this is a very important lesson in one's life.

Initially, when I told him to lift small loads that he could handle, he immediately agreed, because he considered himself eligible to carry out the task.

But when I told him to lift the 200 kg load, he knew that it was beyond his capacity, or in other words, he clearly knew that he was not eligible to carry out that task.

Similarly, in the world of finance, you should determine your "Eligibility index" (EI) meaning what part of your income you can spend without hurting your current and future financial lives. I strongly recommend you to fix a percentage of your income as your EI as it will work for a life time without creating any confusion.

Ganesh asked me how he should determine a percentage and why?

I said, "See, when you fix a part of your income as your EI then every time your income changes you have to calculate your EI. Therefore, with time, you'll go back to your old ways. Therefore, it's always better to fix a percentage as you won't have to revise it each time."

Ganesh looked at me and asked, "Sir, is that the template[5] you have in front of you?

I said, "Yes. This is your homework."

Then I handed it over to him and asked him to fill in the details to arrive at his EI (Eligibility Index) before the next session.

Before concluding, I said, "Ganesh, this template is the second most important template next only to RC template. These two templates are so powerful that they can change anybody's life. So exercise maximum care while working on them and keep them with you for lifetime."

Ganesh nodded.

---

[5]*This is covered more in detail in our MGM 3 day's intensive workshop. For more details visit our website www.abundanceindia.com*

GOLDEN RULE 15

NEVER SIGN A CONTRACT OF SLAVERY

"The world pressures us to buy things we don't need, with money we don't have, to impress people we don't like"

-Rick Warren

Our discussion the following Sunday began. He briefed me about how his budget was panning out and asked me for some advice for situations he had encountered the previous week. After that, he showed me brochure on which a beautiful gated community with 7 towers of residential flats was printed.

He said, "Sir, two of my senior colleagues in the company have signed up for this as they feel it is a good offer and has value for money. The builder is so influential that he is arranging for the loan from a certain bank that offers up to 80% of the value of the flat. Is this a good offer, Sir?"

I smiled at his naivety and said, "Ganesh always remember this - If any one comes to you with an offer to sell something saying that it is a great product with great features, value for money and the like, stay away from them. They have a hidden agenda and they are asking you to sign a "Contract of Slavery". The longer the term, the better for them."

"In the current world, nothing except mother's love comes for free.

Don't fall into such traps. Marketers and sales people will use all their skills and techniques to convince you that you have no choice but to buy their product."

"Your life is made simple. Simply follow the Golden rules of Money and focus on reaching your goals faster so that, you not only have financial freedom but also the freedom of time."

"If by any chance, you fall for such deceptive sales pitches, you will end up being a slave for the rest of your life, like millions of people across the world right now."

I then gave a template to Ganesh and told him to use it in such a situation.

"Learn to politely refuse offers when they don't pass through three stage filters[6] mentioned in this template."

[6] *This is covered more in detail in our MGM 3 day's intensive workshop. For more details visit our website www.abundanceindia.com*

I am mentioning about MGM workshop in the book not with the intention of promoting it but, to bring it to your attention as it has helped thousands of people overcome financial stress to lead a life of freedom and joy.

Ganesh was excited that he got something more valuable.

I told him, "Ganesh study the template thoroughly and see if you can identify bad money decisions that you have made in life so far. Remember, it is a very powerful template."

We concluded the meeting.

GOLDEN RULE 16

DON'T LET OTHERS ROB YOU OF YOUR FUTURE

"He that goes a borrowing goes a sorrowing"
- Benjamin Franklin.

As a practice we started our meeting on time.

I looked at Ganesh and told him. "Ganesh, never let others rob you of your future."

He was taken aback.

He stared at me for few seconds and said. "Sir, I don't understand. How can anyone rob me of my future?

I told him. "Let me explain."

Napoleon Hill in his great book "Think and Grow rich" has mentioned that "without doubt, the most common weakness of all human begins is the habit of leaving their minds open to the negative influence of other people." Most people are not able to live the life of their dreams. They let others rob their future as they are easily influenced by the opinion of the others. They permit every one surrounding them to do their thinking and influence them to buy their products and services irrespective of their needs and desires. This can push one to lifetime slavery.

Generally sales people/agents/brokers from banks, Insurance companies, Real estate companies, chit funds and other lending firms approach people with many offers.

They are all trained to convince people with their skills and techniques to sell their products or services. Their job is to sell and make a living out of that.

Most of the times people end up buying the wrong products or services because they themselves don't understand what they are buying. Their decision is triggered through an emotional chord temporarily controlled by the sales person sitting in front of them.

How to overcome that?

Over the years, through my research, I gathered that one should learn to build his/her financial life on 10 strong pillars. If they are successful in that, their life will be a bed of roses despite the thorns.

Now, what are those 10 pillars?

GOLDEN RULE 17

10 PILLARS

"Learn to build your empire on the firm foundation of the Fundamentals"

- Lou Holtz

"I used to think that successful people are successful because they are highly talented and lucky.

Of course, they are talented. But it is not their talent alone that earned them their riches. They are team players.

They first identify their core strength and analyse what are the other strengths they need to be successful and identify experts in those areas and start associating with them.

We all know the story of the hare and the tortoise. Slow and steady wins the race was the moral. But here is an extension. The rabbit thought for a while and felt that over-confidence and carelessness was the reason for his defeat. So, he called for a race a second time. Sure enough the rabbit ran the race with energy and enthusiasm and won, leaving the turtle far behind proving that the fast and consistent will always beat the slow and steady. Now, the turtle did some thinking and realised that he could never win if the route was the way it was.

He thought for a while and then challenged the rabbit again, but on a slightly different route. The rabbit and the turtle took off at the start line. The rabbit, not to be outwitted, ran all through at top speed until he came to a broad river. He stopped because the finish line was the other side of the river. In the meantime, the turtle trundled along, got into the river, swam across and continued walking to the finish line. This is where you have to understand that identifying your strength matters so much.

However, the story doesn't end here. In the process of racing so many times, the rabbit and the turtle became friends and decided to run the race together. This time the rabbit carried the turtle on the land and the turtle carried the rabbit in the water. They reached the finish line together with greater satisfaction proving that when individually brilliant people come together and share their strengths, success is guaranteed.

After some research, I found that an average man can easily become successful by having a life time association with ten pillars in his/her life (Figure 14). If a person is willing to grow and contribute to the growth of the others in the team, he/she is sure to be surrounded by like-minded people.

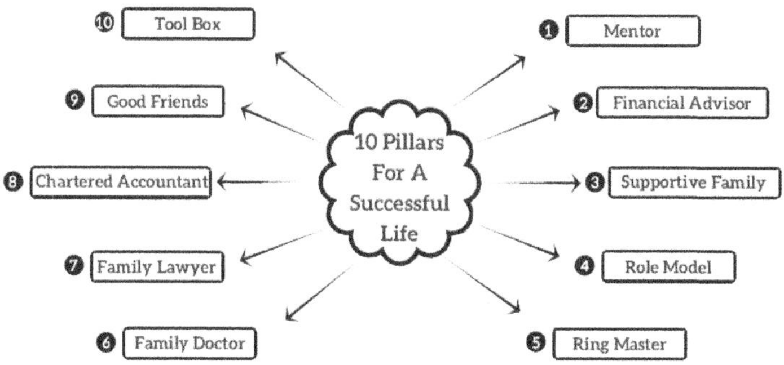

Figure 14 – Pillars of Success

1. Mentor/Coach/Guru:

Take a look at any successful person. It may be a cricketer, an industrialist, a musician or anyone for that matter. Each is sure to have had at least one mentor guiding him/her or who guided him/her at one point of time.

2. Financial Advisor:

A financial advisor is very important in one's life because of the fact that money plays a vital role in an individual's life. It is important that one plans his finances in such a way that he is comfortable today, tomorrow and for the rest of his life.

One has to be prudent in identifying his financial advisor since there is a lot of risk attached to money management. An intelligent financial advisor who has no ulterior motives and who is truly willing to guide you is most certainly a blessing in disguise.

3. Supportive family:

The support of your family is irreplaceable. Without this, it becomes highly difficult for a person to be successful in his life. Family is the backbone for any individual and they appreciate and encourage whether asked or not. Moral, physical, psychological or financial support, they will always be there for you.

4. Role Model:

Having a reference helps one understand a race or an exam or an activity or whatever venture one is taking up better.

Similarly, in life, you need an achiever as your role model who will inspire you to reach your goal much faster.

A mentor or role model can be anyone – someone you know or someone you don't. The important thing is to imbibe those qualities in you that helped them reach their goals, use them as a reference and achieve your goals.

5. Ring Master:

In a circus, you would have witnessed a trainer with a long whip controlling all the wild and untamed animals. He is called the Ring Master.

Similarly, one needs a task master who would hold you accountable for your actions and will ensure that you perform the way you are expected to.

6. Family doctor:

Health is always at the top of your priority list. A family doctor plays an important role in one's life to keep one healthy and fit.

7. Family Lawyer:

You may not have the need to see a doctor or lawyer every day, but when the need arises, they will definitely be of great help.

8. Chartered Accountant:

You may see a CA only towards the end of the year for filing your tax returns or audit. However, it is important to maintain a long term association with your CA to keep yourself constantly updated.

9. Good friend Circle:

A good friend circle is valuable as they will stand by you during your tough times.

10. Tool Box:

Your most worthwhile Tool Box is nothing but your brain. It is what holds all the knowledge and information that will support you throughout."

After explaining about the 10 pillars I asked Ganesh. "Are you clear so far?"

He nodded his head.

Then I told him. "Ganesh, I have taught you enough to be on your own. The 17 Golden rules that you have learnt are the most powerful rules you will not find anywhere because they are born out of my experience. So make sure that you keep your notes safe and review whenever required.

Now you are good to go. Henceforth we shall meet once a quarter to check progress and for further lessons if required."

It was an emotionally charged situation and we concluded.

Macro level Financial Statement of Ganesh (Table 7) is provided on page 155.

2. OUTER GAME OF MONEY

GOLDEN RULE 18

HOW DEEP

"Bad debt is sacrificing your future day needs for your present-day desires"

- Suze Orman

Let us now look at Anil's financial life till this point.

Table 5 – Anil's Financial Statement

Year	2000	2001	2002	2003	2004	2005	2006	2007	2008	2009	2010	2011	2012	2013	2014	2015	2016
Opening Balance	**0**	**107214**	**186931**	**268836**	**324291**	**428136**	**-923062**	**-1297004**	**-1672487**	**-1924394**	**-2107629**	**-2300200**	**-2711379**	**-2825856**	**-2960875**	**-3136473**	**-3378284**
Inflows-																	
Salary + Bonus	400000	440000	484000	532400	715640	858768	944645	1039109	1246931	1371624	1508787	1659665	2157565	2373321	2610654	2871719	3158891
Bank interest		4289	7477	10753													
Income from spouse																	
Total Inflows	**400000**	**444289**	**491477**	**543153**	**715640**	**858768**	**944645**	**1039109**	**1246931**	**1371624**	**1508787**	**1659665**	**2157565**	**2373321**	**2610654**	**2871719**	**3158891**
Outflows-																	
Living expenses	180000	198000	217800	239580	263538	289892	318881	350769	385846	424431	466874	513561	564917	621409	683550	751905	827095
Bike 60K	11786	23572	23572	11786													
Entertainment	48000	84000	102000	122400	146880	176256	211507	253809	304570	365484	438581	526298	631557	757869	909442	1091331	1309597
Clothing	12000	14400	17280	20736	24883	29860	35832	42998	51598	61917	74301	89161	106993	128392	154070	184884	221861
Education	18000	21600	25920	31104	37325	44790	53748	64497	77397	92876	111451	133742	160490	192588	231105	277326	332792
Insurance premium	23000	23000	23000	39000	46800	46800	46800	50700	50700	50700	50700	50700	50700	50700	50700	50700	50700
Car				23092	92369	92369	92369	92369	69277			197933	197933	197933	197933	197933	
Private loan interest							64000	64000	64000	64000	64000	64000	64000	64000	64000	64000	64000
Housing loan							495450	495450	495450	495450	495450	495450	495450	495450	495450	495450	495450
Marriage-self						1530000											
Total Outflows	**292786**	**364572**	**409572**	**487698**	**611795**	**2209966**	**1318587**	**1414593**	**1498838**	**1554859**	**1701357**	**2070845**	**2272041**	**2508341**	**2786251**	**3113530**	**3301495**
Closing Balance	**107214**	**186931**	**268836**	**324291**	**428136**	**-923062**	**-1297004**	**-1672487**	**-1924394**	**-2107629**	**-2300200**	**-2711379**	**-2825856**	**-2960875**	**-3136473**	**-3378284**	**-3520888**

As of Dec 2016, he was ₹50 Lakhs deep in debt with no sign of getting out anytime soon. (As per Table 5 plus personal borrowings)

He was completely stressed out. He knew he had to do something but had no idea what? Looking at him, I remembered the time when I was bankrupt. The only difference now was – I knew a way out of it for him.

I first analysed his situation and asked him, "Do you know HOW DEEP you are?" I pointed out all the small and big things to show him how serious his situation was. I said, "Getting into debt is easy. It's like getting fat. But getting out is hard. It is like becoming thin. It requires a lot of discipline and determination. You have lost a lot of precious time. You will now have to leverage time to make up for the lost time." He quietly nodded and said, "What do I have to do now, Sir?"

I told him to not think too far ahead just yet. He would have to break down his problem into small fragments and conquer them one by one. I gave him a reassuring smile and said," I will guide you at every step."

My smile comforted him and made him a little more confident. He breathed.

"The first thing is to do things on a day to day basis by taking charge and pushing things; not waiting for things to happen."

Then I gave him a 6-point revival program as follows :

1. Absolutely no borrowing money for the rest of his life.

2. Repay debt not month on month but in one go and get out of slavery.

He was stunned. "WHAT! How can I do that, Sir?"

I smiled and said," Patience. It's all possible."

3. Take one month leave from your company and start your business.

Anil couldn't contain his astonishment. He exclaimed," Business? What business, Sir? I can't come close to the B of business even!"

I asked him to wait till I finish before jumping to conclusions. He kept quiet.

4. Play the money game to win.

5. Educate yourself on a day to day basis by reading about good money habits and successful people. Interact with Ganesh whenever possible and catch up with him in the journey of personal finance.

I told him to make a note of all this because it was going to be a long list. He opened his laptop when I said," No, don't use a laptop. Write it all in your own handwriting. It may not seem like a huge deal now but the impact it creates later will surprise you." He started writing.

6. Be grateful for all that you have now.

Never curse your money, your company, your boss, your colleagues, family members, friends, relatives etc. because they have been supporting you in life. It was your foolishness that you fell into a trap. So don't hold others responsible.

Start thanking money, your employer and your boss for keeping you alive by paying you month on month.

Learn to respect money and people.

Make a list of your strengths and weaknesses to know your KRAs. Also note down questions/doubts as and when you get them.

Meet me after 15 days. By then, I will have a program designed for you.

GOLDEN RULE 19

LADDER UP TO GROUND ZERO

"There can be no freedom or beauty about a home life that depends on borrowing and debt"
-Henrik Ibsen

Anil had his book ready with all details as discussed during the 2nd meeting.

I glanced through his book and I paid more attention to the list of his strengths.

What caught my attention was that most of his relatives were into weaving silk sarees and dress material business and some of them were exporters as well.

I asked Anil about his relationship with family and relatives. He said they were all very closely knit and always had each other's backs.

I asked him how many of them he knew personally. He said, " About 30 such families. My parents know a lot more though."

I asked him about his connections with his wife's relatives. He said, "I am not close to many relatives from her side, she is."

I also asked him if his parents and wife knew about the mess he was in. He said that they knew that he had taken a huge housing loan but didn't know of the sufferings that followed.

"Does your father have a good financial background, Anil?"

He cleared his throat and said that his father was working for an automobile industry. On a fateful day he met with a serious accident and lost his right leg. Since then, he had no confidence in himself and always chose to stay at home. Ever since, his mother was taking care of the family.

"What does your mother do to finance the expenses of the family?"

"She runs a small business which caters to the needs of working women in our neighborhood, Sir."

That gave me an idea but I didn't voice it to Anil yet.

I told Anil to make a list of about 20 relatives of his and come with his wife and mother for the next meeting.

Anil looked a little uncomfortable.

I comforted him by saying that he need not worry about small things when he is set to crack a bigger one. Also, by taking family members into confidence, half the stress will vanish.

Anil came with his mother and wife for the next meeting.

After exchanging pleasantries with them I explained to them about Anil's predicament and how he had been suffering partly because of his lenders and partly because he had to hide his sufferings from his family behind a happy face.

Both women started to cry. I reassured them by saying that I had already devised a way out of this mess for them.

His mother said, "Can I ask you a question?"

"Sure, please do."

"Sir, from the looks of it, you seem like someone with a lot of experience. But how can we trust you? Please forgive me if I seem blunt but I am just trying to understand. We had a neighbor by the name Janardhan whom we trusted blindly but later we understood that he had conned us.

Anil shot out telling his mother to keep quiet and stop asking such stupid questions.

I intervened and told Anil it was perfectly alright.

I thanked his mother for being straight forward by asking me that question.

I went on to tell her about myself and my roller coaster ride from rags to riches, how I met Gopalakrishnan at the time when I most needed the guidance and support who later on turned into a mentor and now my Guru for life. He is a selfless man with zero expectation.

"That is why I do what I do. Having felt the pain and humiliation, I want to help others out of it. For those who haven't gotten in, help them steer clear of it.

After she heard me, she apologized.

Now, she was clear about my intentions and wholeheartedly thanked me for helping her son.

His wife who was silent all along said she can part with her jewelry to clear a part their loan.

Anil was very upset that his wife was offering her jewelry which was so close to her heart. I saw all of them come together in a time of need and it warmed my heart. I said, "Don't worry anymore, you are in good hands. I will surely get you out of this."

I asked Anil's mother if her relatives can help their family financially. She said that they had a good relationship with all her relatives but they had never taken any financial assistance from them. They would surely lend a helping hand, if help was sought.

I asked her to make a list of 12 relatives who would lend them ₹500,000 each without talking ill of them to others.

Anil's mother nodded and said, "Yes, we can manage to find 12 such relatives. But, Sir, should we really seek their help?"

I told Anil's mother that I had been supporting and guiding people get out of debt and slavery for many years. And I was successful each time because I analyzed their strengths and weaknesses and found ways to capitalise their strength and mitigate the weakness.

In Anil's case, his strength is his family – they were both wealthy and helpful. She nodded in agreement.

I then asked her about her business.

"After my husband lost his leg in a tragic accident, I was desperately in need of money to cater to the medical bills as well as the family needs. Like the famous adage goes – "Necessity is the mother of invention"- my desperate needs gave birth to my business. I support working women in different ways based on their requirements" (I am not discussing about their business here to protect their identity as it is a well-known brand).

Anyway, I was happy and convinced that I had a brilliant fool-proof idea.

I told them to make a list of people whom they trust, meet them and collect ₹60 Lakhs from them at zero percent interest in the next one month and then meet me. Also I asked them to inform them that they will return the money in 18 months' time.

"We can arrange that. Also Sir, I do not wish to bring this to my husband's notice", she said worriedly. I told her, "I'd suggest that you take your time and tell him instead of keeping him completely in the dark."

And with that the meeting was concluded.

GOLDEN RULE 20

CRUSH YOUR DEBT TO DEATH

"Get smart and kill debt mercilessly before it kills you"
-R Subramanya CFP

To my surprise, Anil called me a week later and told me that they had the money and wanted to know when he could meet me.

I checked my calendar and told him to meet me after 2 days.

"Should I come alone or should I get my mother and wife along, Sir?"

I told him to get them along.

Anil, his mother and wife visited me 2 days later.

After exchanging the casual pleasantries, Anil's mother told me that she had ₹60 Lakhs plus her savings of ₹4 Lakhs with them and wanted to know how to proceed further.

I was genuinely surprised. I asked, "How did you manage to get the money so fast?"

Anil's mother said, "On our way back home the other day, we were discussing different possibilities when Anil suddenly reminded me of my childhood friend who is originally from Kerala but settled down in Bangalore. She's as close to me as anyone can get. Although, I have never asked her for any favour, I know for a fact that she'd help if need be. So, on reaching home, I called her and asked if I could meet her. She gladly said yes. I met her and I was really happy to see her after so long. But she could see past that and asked me what was bothering me. I explained everything to her for 2 reasons – 1. Hoping she'd help me. 2. To help myself by getting it off my chest. She thought for a while and then said, 'Instead of me giving you ₹500,000 and you going to eleven others, I will give you the entire amount as I have deposits which I don't need anytime soon.' It's unbelievable how God helps you in myriad different ways and forms."

I listened attentively and said, "That's really good. You have made my work simpler too by obtaining the cash from a single source as creating a repayment schedule for one is far better than doing it for 12 people."

I began to explain the next course of action as follows -

1. You can park ₹64 Lakhs in a liquid mutual fund. Consider ₹4 Lakhs as your emergency fund for the next 1 year till we stabilize your business. Other ₹60 Lakhs you will be withdrawing as and when you require on the basis of cash flow forecast which will be provided to you. But, never keep your money in the bank. You will lose money if you do so.

2. Clear both Housing loan and car loan completely. Usually I don't advise people to close their housing loan in a short period of time from the date of borrowing. But, in your case I want you to close it immediately. (for reasons beyond the scope of this book)

3. Anil should take one month's leave and work on a business plan under my guidance.

4. Recruit and train people to run business in different locations.

5. Appoint an accountant who will work as per my instructions.

If you follow these 5 steps religiously you will be financially free within the next 4 years."

Anil was shocked. "Did I hear you right, Sir? Did you say 4 years?"

I said, "Yes. You heard it right. Immediately go to the bank and close your loans. They may try to convince you to keep it going or they may offer you more funding. Simply ignore them, mercilessly kill both loans. Get out of slavery and come back to me as a free man."

They nodded their heads. I went on.

The things I said, the way I said it, filled him with unbounded enthusiasm. He braced himself for the last but the most important leg of the race.

After my instructions Anil held my hand between both his hands and thanked me profusely. I patted his back and said, "Anil, I am only a coach. You are the player on the field. I can take the horse to water, I can't make it drink unless it is thirsty. Similarly, I have parted my knowledge to you. Now, it's your turn to use it wisely and make the most of it. Remember, success is his, who stops at nothing till he crosses and goes through the finishing line."

I could see his eyes beaming with confidence and determination. I was happy that I was making a difference in his life.

As we were discussing I could see that Anil's mother was restless. When I asked her as to what was bothering her, she hesitantly asked me. "Sir, why do you say that we lose money by depositing in the bank?"

I told her that her money will work for the bank and the government and not for her. So it isn't a wise idea to deposit money in the bank.

She looked confused. I then calculated and showed her the Table 6.

(Values are not accurate as they are rounded off for easy understanding)

Deposit Amount	Interest Rate	No, Of Years	Value
4,00,000	7%	3	4,90,000
Inflation @ 6%			68,000
Value after Inflation			4,22,000
Tax Bracket @ 10%			9,000
Value after Tax			4,13,000

Table 6 – ROI on FD

"Imagine you are depositing ₹4,00,000/- in the bank at 7% (taken as an example) for 3 years. Bank will give you an FD certificate wherein they will mention the deposit amount as ₹4 Lakhs, Interest rate 7% and maturity amount after 3 years would be ₹4,90,017/-"

I went on, "But, What happens in reality is entirely different. Year on year money keeps going down in value. Value of money keeps reducing over a period of time due to inflation."

They all listened very attentively.

I went on, "10 years ago cost of 1 kg of rice was ₹17 and today it is ₹70. This is because value of money is going down not because the measure of 1 kg has changed. In other words our purchasing power keeps reducing. If we purchase, say, a pen for ₹100 today, we may have to pay about ₹107 for the same one year from now considering inflation @ 7%."

I asked them if they understood. They all nodded in unison wanting me to go on.

Anil's mother gaped at me with this new fed information. She said in disbelief, "But, we have always thought that money grew in value when deposited in banks."

I explained to her, "People turn a blind eye to the details. Once they see the words- EARN INTEREST OF 7% - they don't care much about the process. Like in the above example, you would be looking at ₹4,90,000 and seeing ₹90,000 as the extra money earned. But in truth, of that, ₹68,000 vanishes without a trace due to inflation and ₹9,000 will be your tax outgo since you come under 10% slab. We are unaware of these things as no one educated us about money matters." So instead of ₹90,000 you will only get

₹13,000. Remember, longer the term more the loss. Your capital itself can get eroded.

I also made it a point to tell them that banks are not bad. It is one's own naivety or smartness that makes a difference. Banks are useful in many ways; we just need to know how to use it to our advantage.

Anil asked, "What do we do with our savings then, Sir?"

I told them that savers are losers. If one wants to win, he must invest*.

As he was about to ask me about how to go about investments I cut him short saying that he should now focus only on the 5 point program given to him.

They looked at each other for a second and immediately turned to me and thanked me for the support.

We closed our meeting for the day.

**Investments and investment strategies are not part of this book as it is exhaustive. (For the benefit of my readers I am writing a book on simple investment principles to create and sustain wealth). Readers are advised to use these as guidelines as no two individuals will have the same situation, hence strategies cannot be simply implemented to the letter. For professional help you may get in touch with us or other financial advisers for a holistic approach towards your financial life. Remember, any experiment with money without knowledge or professional guidance will be expensive.*

GOLDEN RULE 21

FAST TRACK TO FINANCIAL FREEDOM

"You have but one life and you can't be multiplied,
But your money can be"

- R Subramanya CFP

Anil accompanied by his mother and wife was on time as usual.

I was happy to see them follow my instructions to the dot. It showed that they trusted me.

Anil's mother took out some papers from her bag and gave them to Anil. Anil, with all his excitement, showed me those papers. Those were the papers discharging him from slavery, finally breaking free from the shackles that had bound him for years now - he had cleared both vehicle and housing loans completely.

Next few minutes they shared their experience of going to the bank and their discussions with the bank officials and their reaction etc.

I felt really good looking at how they had started to find solutions rather than focus on problems.

I said, "Now that barrier had been crossed, are you ready to face the next one?"

They eagerly said yes.

I told Anil, "You should take two month's leave from your company to do three things.

1. First month, be with your mother and help her and at the same time learn about her business and generate additional amount of profits equivalent to a minimum of your monthly expense.

"This is your first challenge", I said. I am fixing a target. But I am not telling you any specific path to reach the same. Find your path. Pave it. Reach your goals.

They looked confused. "All this while I was working on creating the context. Now, I am telling you the sequence in which you should be working. But, how to do it is to be decided by you. With all the knowledge I have imparted to you, I am sure you can ace it."

I explained to them why, what I think is possible to build their confidence. "I have the advantage of over 4 decades of experience as a Businessman and a financial adviser. I can easily understand businesses and the risks and rewards attached to it. I have understood your business. It has great potential. I also know the profit margins that you are currently making and how it can be increased by doing simple things. What you have failed to identify is the potential for leverage and that is the tool I want you to use to your advantage. It may be overwhelming but stay focused. Solutions maybe be staring from right under your nose. You just need to know the right place to look."

I told Anil, "I am going to share 3 templates with you. Make sure that you spend quality time, quickly understand your business and gather all data in the templates and send it to me. Using this, I will create:

a. Business model
b. Cash flow forecast
c. Resource planning and
d. Systems & Processes.

With these you will have to create complete set of documents about each and every aspect of your business."

Anil asked, "Sir, why the documentation?"

I replied. "For Fast Trak Freedom, You must learn to think BIG. I will not allow you to run the business as a

Solo-Entrepreneur, like your mother".

You have to think, act and behave like a true businessman. I am sure it will take time but you have an innate talent to adopt to dynamic surroundings. The problem right now isn't how you can do that but that you don't even know your hidden potential. Once you identify that within yourself, you'll get answers to questions which seemed impossible earlier. Do you know that there is a Millionaire sleeping within? I am here to help you awaken that. So, "AWAKEN THE MILLIONAIRE WITHIN"[7](ATMW)

Anil was now so charged up that if someone were to touch him, he'd feel the electric current pass through him.

The second thing that I asked Anil to do was –

1. To understand your mother's business completely.

"Anil, do you know the fastest way to teach someone to swim?"

Anil said, "By sending them to coaching classes."

I smiled and shook my head at the generic answer and said, "In that case, have you tried grabbing and throwing someone into water?"

It dawned on him. He agreed.

[7]*ATMW is covered more in detail in our MGM 3 day's intensive workshop. It is our passion to build a millionaire mindset for individuals to live their dreams. For more details visit our website www.abundanceindia.com*

I continued, "Similarly, I am not going to teach you step by step of how a business works. Instead, I'm throwing you in, it's your choice to either sink or swim. Either way, you'll learn the nuances of business which no one could've ever taught you."

He didn't look confident. I went on, "No one taught your mother how to run a business but she is doing a pretty good job. If she can do it, you with a better educational foundation, can surely do better. Also, you will have your mother to support you in case you need some guidance. Only drawback I see is that you are short of time. That is just about a month not only to learn the business but also to create documents of your business."

So, in your own interest, you must grasp things fast. I have given you sufficient information and guidance to reach your first target and I promise you that it will change your life forever.

2. Recruit 10 more people and train them to run the business the way your mother is doing currently.

Till now, Anil's mother and wife were quiet but attentive. I looked at his mother and understood that she was not very comfortable.

I told her to believe in her son and follow my instructions.

She nodded.

I asked her if she had trustworthy people in her team.

She said, "Sir, I have 2 women who are highly dedicated.
I told her to do 2 things in the next 30 days.

1. Get about 10 people like her trusted employees.

2. Identify and establish 10 new locations for her business.

Can that be done?

She said, "Yes, it is possible but Sir, I am not able to cater to the demands in my current area of business. Can we not expand it here itself."

I told her, "Yes, you can do it. But as a strategy, it is better to spread the base."

I told her that she must be proud that she had not only created a business which took care of her family but also was going to rewrite her destiny forever.

"I have helped hundreds of salaried people find and establish their own businesses depending on their strengths to liberate themselves from financial mess. Not every situation is same. Every individual is different. We need to carefully study their financial life and device a workable solution. From my long experience I can only say one thing - There is no money problem that cannot be solved. Particularly salary class have a unique strength which they don't recognise. That strength can liberate any individual if he/she can adopt the strategies that I am discussing here in this book.

Listening to me, She said, "Yes sir. If you say so, we will do it."

I told her that she was very resourceful.

She just smiled and thanked me.

Things started moving the way we had planned but with few small hiccups here and there.

Anil had taken leave. He was completely immersed in his mother's business. Since he was a free man who didn't have to worry about the burden of monthly EMI and tough targets from his employer, he was enjoying his work.

He was regularly updating me of the progress. After a month we all met. I could see that Anil was more enthusiastic that things were going good.

He said that, "Sir, I am thoroughly enjoying my work. I should have thought of this earlier. But, the idea didn't strike me."

I said, "Better late than never. I am happy that you love your job. That means you respect your job and it's a good sign. Remember, gratitude is the way to Abundance."

He told me. "Sir, I am doing everything you have instructed me to but I failed in one."

"I knew what he was referring to. I told him wait till we came to that point in a while."

He nodded his head.

Then I asked his mother about the new workforce.

She said. Sir, we could identify 8 people who are ready to work. I will get two more in a week's time.

I told Anil. From tomorrow you and your mother have to start training new people exactly the way you learnt your business except for finances. You keep managing that till you get an accountant for the job.

Use the documents and stick to them. Any changes you need to make discuss them with your mother and take her approval, make a note of them and then implement.

He said. Sir, "I am lucky that I was trained on most of these activities and I am really grateful for my company and my boss."

I said, "Anil don't you see the power of being grateful."

He nodded his head.

We went on to discuss more about his business and their roles.

Anil asked me, "Sir, Can I involve my wife also into this?"

I said, "Why not? In that case, you will have an in-house accountant. Let her handle the finances."

They were happy at how their thinking had changed from finding problems to identifying solutions.

Finally we touched upon cash flow statement. All the figures looked good. But, additional profit of ₹40000/- equivalent to his monthly expenses was less by ₹15,000/-

Anil looked at me and said, "Although I learnt a lot, I am disappointed with my performance because I know I could've done better. Give me another month and I will make up for the shortfall and earn an extra of ₹25,000/".

I gave him a stern look indicating that there was no room for inefficiencies this time.

His mother who was witnessing all those said. "Sir, thank you for your support. Though I had my own fears I am now confident. We feel blessed to have someone like you to guide us."

I told her that at times I may be tough on Anil and the rest of them but, in their own interest.

She said, "Sir you are our Guru please guide us; we will blindly follow your instructions."

We closed our meeting for that day by scheduling a final meeting to tie all lose ends.

Final meeting

Anil along with his family entered my office. All of them were enthusiastic as ever. The stress and tension on their faces in those initial days was replaced with happiness and peace. After going through the records, I was satisfied that both theirs and my efforts were bearing fruits. They were progressing well.

Then I asked them about the training program they had started for the new recruits. "How are they responding? Are they suitable?"

Anil said. "Sir, except for one lady who left due to her personal issues, others are all good and interested in the work".

I said. "Okay, that means we have 7 ladies. Here is what you do. Withdraw ₹3 Lakhs and invest in resources for the second territory and hand it over to one of your old employee with one new employee to assist her. But make sure that the new business should be equal to your current business and not less".

I told Anil, "Anil it is your job to train them and get them accustomed to the new systems".

Anil said, "Sir the good news is that they love our new system as it saves them both time and effort."

I said, "Good, that is encouraging. So, are you all clear about what we have discussed so far?"

They nodded in unison.

I told them, "Look, you had a business. Now you have learnt to duplicate your business. That means you have doubled your business and with that your profit will also double or more. Doesn't this make you happy and proud?"

They nodded in unison again. But this time with a big smile.

I went on. "This is the rule of the game. I have shared with you all the templates and check lists to assist you. You have already created a set of business process documents. All these are gift from me. They are your real assets known only to the three of you. Make sure you respect and protect them. Never lose them."

They got emotional when they realised that this would be their last meeting with me on a regular basis. I allowed them some time and told them, "I know what it is to feel trapped in poverty and slavery. No one should ever have to face that. I have tried my best to train you. Now how you use it is on you. I have shown you the path and given you a road map. In case you face any challenge let me know."

Anil's mother looked at me and asked, "Sir, are you going to stop interacting with us?"

I told her that since the ground work has been done, so much of interaction would not be necessary henceforth. However, should they encounter any challenges; I was just a call away.

They thanked me profusely and left.

Anil religiously followed the road map to financial freedom I had prepared for him. He added the 3rd territory in the 4th month, 2 more in the 5th month, another 2 in the 6th month, 1 in the 7th month, 1 in the 10th month, and established 10 new territories in the next 15 months.

All territories started producing desired results. They grew by leaps and bounds. It gave me immense joy and satisfaction watching them grow. It's one of those feelings that I can't put in words.

Anil being tech savvy introduced simple methods to train, monitor and measure progress of each and every territory on a day to day basis. As per the master plan surplus amount was regularly invested under my guidance. In 2 years 2 months they could create a corpus of a little more than ₹62 Lakhs.

When I broke that news to them, they jumped up in joy.

They were at my office the next morning. Anil said with a lot of excitement. "Sir, now that we have enough cash, we'd like to organize an event to thank my mother's friend who lent us ₹60 Lakhs." Little did I know that they planned to surprise me there. They returned the ₹60 Lakhs to the kind lady along with a silk saree and a gold chain to express their gratitude. They then called me on stage. Knowing that I don't prefer to accept gifts, they wholeheartedly thanked me. Little did they know that this was more special than any gift.

It was all very touching. A young boy who was trapped in debt with no hopes of freedom could overcome all that to achieve freedom in just 4 years. I call it "FAST TRACK TO FINANCIAL FREEDOM".

I felt humbled knowing that I could bring this difference in his life. It feels great to see Anil and his family doing so well and leading a life of their dreams.

The reason for me to share Anil's story here is for two simple reasons;

1. No one is born to lead a life of poverty or slavery. "Life is a Gift from God" and no individual is sent to this world with a label of poverty or slavery.

2. Any human being can get rich irrespective of his past because *"There is no Poverty in God's land."* All that one needs is good money habits or a good financial adviser to help him inculcate those habits.

My Mission is to reach out to every Indian directly or indirectly to empower them to take financial literacy seriously to fulfill all their desires.

I pray to Almighty to grant everyone a life full of ABUNDANCE, freedom and joy.

Hope our paths cross again soon.

God bless you all!

Table 7 – Ganesh's Financial Freedom Statement

Year	2000	2001	2002	2003	2004	2005	2006	2007	2008	2009	2010	2011	2012	2013	2014	2015	2016
Opening Balance	**8600**	**235900**	**512690**	**871284**	**1305005**	**1929258**	**2741189**	**3709726**	**2494638**	**2675342**	**3707617**	**5145059**	**6858418**	**9109237**	**12004388**	**15495458**	**19687999**
Inflows-																	
Salary + Bonus	370000	407000	447700	492470	671717	806060	886666	975333	1170400	1287440	1416184	1557802	2025143	2227657	2450423	2695465	2965011
Income from Assets		23590	76904	130693	195751	289389	411178	185486	124732	133767	444914	617407	823010	1366386	1800658	2324319	2953200
Income from spouse										39000	42900	47190	51909	57100	62810	69091	76000
Total Inflows	**370000**	**430590**	**524604**	**623163**	**867468**	**1095449**	**1297845**	**1160819**	**1295132**	**1460207**	**1903998**	**2222399**	**2900062**	**3651142**	**4313891**	**5088874**	**5994211**
Outflows-																	
Family diety 1%	3700	4070	4477	4925	6717	8061	8867	9753	11704	12874	14162	15578	20251	22277	24504	26955	29650
Charity 1%	3700	4070	4477	4925	6717	8061	8867	9753	11704	12874	14162	15578	20251	22277	24504	26955	29650
Living expenses 20%	74000	81400	89540	98494	134343	161212	177333	195067	234080	257488	283237	311560	405029	445531	490085	539093	593002
Entertainment 4%	14800	16280	17908	19699	26869	32242	35467	39013	46816	51498	56647	62312	81006	89106	98017	107819	118600
Clothing 2%	7400	8140	8954	9849	13434	16121	17733	19507	23408	25749	28324	31156	40503	44553	49008	53909	59300
Education 2%	7400	8140	8954	9849	13434	16121	17733	19507	23408	25749	28324	31156	40503	44553	49008	53909	59300
Insurance premium	11700	11700	11700	11700	11700	11700	11700	11700	11700	11700	11700	11700	11700	20300	20300	20300	20300
Bike loan							21608	21608	21608								
Sister'smarriage								2000000									
Marriage-self									700000								
Pilgrimage	20000	20000	20000	30000	30000	30000	30000	50000	30000	30000	30000	30000	30000	50000	50000	50000	50000
Car loan														17394	17394	17394	17394
Total Outflows	**142700**	**153800**	**166010**	**189441**	**243215**	**283518**	**329307**	**2375907**	**1114427**	**427932**	**466555**	**509041**	**649243**	**755991**	**822821**	**896333**	**977197**
Closing Balance	**235900**	**512690**	**871284**	**1305005**	**1929258**	**2741189**	**3709726**	**2494638**	**2675342**	**3707617**	**5145059**	**6858418**	**9109237**	**12004388**	**15495458**	**19687999**	**24705013**

AWAKEN THE MILLIONAIRE WITHIN

R Subramanya and Abundance India Training invite you and your family members to avail this Financial Health Check as a complimentary offer.

For Registration and other information go to **www.abundanceindia.com.**

Use Code - **AIFHC18**
When you register.

(You can also use your book receipt or special promotion code to avail this offer)

---

*The offer is open to all purchases of ***"Awaken the Millionaire Within"*** by R Subramanya. Original proof of purchase is required. The offer is limited to Financial Health Check (FHC), and your registration is subject to availability of time slot and schedule. This is a limited time offer must be completed by the date shown on the website www.abundanceindia.com. The value of this free admission for you and your family is $ 99.5, as of April 2018. Corporate or organisational purchases may not use one book to enrol more than one person. While participants will be responsible for their travel and other costs, admission to the program is complimentary. Participants in the FHC are under no additional financial obligation whatsoever to Abundance India or R Subramanya. Abundance India reserves the right to refuse admission to anyone it believes may disrupt the program.

Author's Appeal

Even in my wildest dreams, I never thought that I'd become a Financial advisor. Back then being a Mechanical Engineer, commerce was Greek and Latin to me. But, Life has its own way of teaching us things. The five major dips that I had in my life taught me that it is a must for everyone to be aware of money matters.

What started as a hobby became my passion and eventually my profession. To me it is a noble profession. My Mission is to help millions and millions of people lead a spectacular life without having to go through the struggle that I went through.

Like they say-"It's smarter to learn from someone else's mistake rather than make your own."

In over 40 years I have seen many uneducated people have better financial acumen than even some of the University toppers. Therefore I understood that even literates are not financially literate. Knowing what the pain, humiliation and suffering feels like I wish that no one will ever have to feel the same. From this thought, this book was born. My Vision is to reach out to as many people as possible through this book. So I humbly appeal to you, my readers to join hands with me and support me in this cause.

You may reach out to me at rs@abundanceindia.com.

Made in the USA
Monee, IL
13 September 2026

62975271R00104